"The need to know more is the need to be more...so I can give more."

'Lolu Ogunmade, 2017

# MindShift
## Unleashing Your Creative Essence

**OMOLOLU O. OGUNMADE**

PYXIDIA HOUSE PUBLISHERS

**MindShift:** Unleashing Your Creative Essence
Copyright© 2017 by Omololu O. Ogunmade.

Request for information on this title should be addressed to

Omololu O. Ogunmade
Lagos, Nigeria
Email: loluogunmade@yahoo.com; loluogunmade@gmail.com
+234 802 303 9928   +234 708 808 0339.

**Library of Congress Cataloging-in-Publication Data**

Omololu O. Ogunmade
**Mindshift:** Unleaching Your Creative Essence
ISBN-13: 978-1-946530-00-4 (Paperback)
ISBN-10: 1-946530-00-X (Paperback)
1. Success - Psychology - Non-fiction  1. Title
Library of Congress Control Number: 2017901064

Edited by Winnie Aduayi

Published in Dallas Texas by Pyxidia House Publishers. A registered trademark of Pyxidia Concept llc.  www.pyxidiahouse.com  info@pyxidiahouse.com

Printed in the United States of America

# DEDICATION

This book is dedicated to my wife, Oluwatoyin and our awesome twins, Orinayo and her brother, Fikunayomi. The coming of Oluwatoyin into my life over two decades ago set the stage for the shift in my life and the arrival of our children four and a half years ago sealed the deal for this work. It was thus just a matter of time.

I love you all much more than I could ever say.

This is for you.

# FOREWORD

I have had to ponder my thoughts in putting pen to paper on this foreword, having been challenged both by the ideas this book propagates, and the prognosis it recommends; that is, the innate demand for contemplation and thought processing in our "doings" and the self-belief that comes with the understanding that follows. My new 'knowing', that every action demands a contemplative thought process in order to achieve a better result than ever before, had me linger a while, in writing this foreword.

'Lolu has dared to reflect and document what most would consider their inner turmoil, or perhaps a crisis of identity; where it would have been easier to flow with your thoughts like ocean currents and hope it lands you in your utopia. As the author himself put it in the preface, *"I am compelled to add this compendium of my thoughts and meditations to the wealth of materials available out there from the stand point of the ordinary person, who has grappled with his own mind for over two decades. I have searched within myself, my person, for answers to how and why I am the person who I have become."*

Mindshift, is a compendium of the thoughts of the author, on why we are limited in our everyday lives, why the challenges of everyday living appear to get the better of us and how our creative essence, that all conquering force can be unleashed to birth a happier you. It is not about mind over matter, but that there is an inner person in all of us, with cognitive ability that provides us with unique insight and understanding into all our challenges and the answers to them. That inner you, when groomed to rise and overshadow the noise and distractions that confront us daily refines and unveils the real you.

Again, as Lolu puts it, *"The decisions we make are based on the programming our minds have gone through in time and on circumstances that we face. It follows that the quality of our decisions which will determine to a large extent the quality of our lives, depend on the environment we are continuously exposed to".*

Mindshift, in my view, is an amazing gift from a man who has taken time out to evaluate himself and his essence, identify the drivers that have brought him to his present, the obstacles that have stood in the way of his aspirations and how they would or could have been overcome. Indeed, with Mindshift there is nothing new under the sun. This book is a periscope into what could be, if our thoughts and processes were rightly calibrated.

Written in the simplest of prose, and referencing everyday challenges, it certainly will bring out a better you.

I hope you experience the shift that takes you to the next base in our continuing march to self-realization.

*Osahon Idemudia*

# CONTENTS

# PREFACE

The literary world is filled with a lot of books on the mind and its workings. Majority of these books, I believe, have been written by experts in philosophy, psychology, religion and business or wealth creation. Thus, the world is not lacking in material to help anyone interested in the workings of the human mind.

However, I am compelled to add this compendium of my thoughts and meditations to the wealth of materials available out there from the stand point of the ordinary person who has grappled with his own mind for over two decades. I have searched within myself, my person, for answers to how and why I am the person who I have become.

This book is therefore a result of the journey I have been through and the processing that I am yet undergoing. My hope is that the principles that I share in this book from a deeply personal angle, which are already established and tested, will impact the reader and bring about what I describe as a 'mindshift'.

I find it necessary to add this book to the volume of work already available, because from my experience, people are searching for easy to apply, everyday principles that will transform their lives. People are quite uninterested in academic pontifications and esoteric philosophies that are irrelevant to day to day living, though they sound good in the classrooms and symposium halls. Life is dynamic and change is constantly happening. The implication of this is that readers today are looking for something different in a book when compared with readers from a couple of decades ago.

There is a sense of connect that comes from learning from the practical experience of another person. This connect does not happen when the same principles and concepts are presented in purely academic formats. What I will be sharing with you therefore represents the outcome of about thirty eight years of my mind's development in the very cognitive part of my life to date. It is the story of a young boy who became a young man who always saw the need to be different, but did not understand the essence of it.

In 1998, based on my perception of business as a marketing executive in a courier service company, and my dream to start my own businesses, I coined a mantra, "there is nothing new under the sun, but the same old things can be done differently." I did not know at the time that what had been inspired in me through that mantra was the definition of who I am as an individual. I describe myself as a non-conformist who has learnt to work seamlessly with the system. I came to believe that new business in the world, going forward, will be based on the re-innovation and modification of what already exists.

The frontiers of business, technology and other spheres of endeavor and enterprise, in my view, have already been established. All new discoveries will basically move these

11

frontiers backwards and will be adaptations of what is already in use based on new thinking. This much has been proven more pointedly in the information technology and social media industry.

Therefore, in the pages of this book I will be laying out, in some respects, familiar principles and concepts that I know can help you find answers to your questions through the anticipated impact of this book on you...a Mindshift.

# Chapter 1

## A LOOK BACK IN TIME

*"Yesterday is history, today is the present, a gift from God..."*

There is an old saying that teaches that knowing where we are coming from is a vital factor in determining where we are going. This is relevant to the objective of writing this book, because wherever you are now on the journey of mind development has historical backgrounds. What has been programmed or stored up in your mind through time is what is responsible for who you are today.

### A Product of Environment

We are said to be products of several life factors and one of these is the environment we are brought up in. Environmental realities go very far in shaping the people's perception, based on the mindset they develop. As children we are basically dependent on our parents, guardians, and other adults around us, who create different environments for us based on their preferences. The mind of a child picks up images and information that eventually shape character traits exhibited by the child as growth progresses. This, of course, is separate from hereditary traits passed down through the genes from parents. The child becomes a young adult whose rational faculties kick in to make informed decisions on life issues.

The decisions we make are based on the programming our minds have gone through in time and on circumstances that we face. It follows then that the quality of our decisions, which will determine to a large extent the quality of our lives depend on the environment we are continuously exposed to. I have begun my discussion in this book from the perspective of environmental impacts on mind development, because people are not brought up in a vacuum; and because people grow to adulthood with contributions to mind programming from different sources. It becomes imperative to highlight the need for the individual who wishes to take a new direction in life to recognize this crucial factor. You may not have been in control of the circumstances of your upbringing, but you have full control of what happens from now on.

My father and mother had six children together through the late sixties to the early eighties. I am the third of the six; and growing up in the seventies I noticed that my dad had a protective shell around his children, which was somewhat unusual to the culture we were born into. It is true that we lived in communal settings, where as a child, you were brought up by the entire adult population you were exposed to. However, my dad made it clear to us, and to the extended family too, that his children would be brought up just the way he wanted. This attitude of his made a strong impression on me, and my siblings too, I guess.

In my discussions with him, as I grew up, he made it clear to me that he understood the need for him to establish a life pattern for us to model. He added that we would eventually have to establish our own standards as adults, but once we had imbibed the basics from him, he could be confident that we would make the right choices going forward. Needless to say, my dad, bless his soul, was not a perfect man. He always made a point of telling us how he was also brought up by a strict disciplinarian father, who at a time put him in the care of a 'master' to further instill focus and discipline into him.

However, as great a dad as he was, my dad was a middle class banker who was exchanging his time and knowledge of banking for a salary. Therefore, at his best, he could only impart the importance of a 'good' education to us, with the target being to finish with good grades. That in his view would present us with better chances to get good jobs, so we could live the same middle class lives with the hope to make it big eventually. The problem was that the family struggled, and he eventually left the bank frustrated to start life as an entrepreneur. This was something he had never been trained for, and which he did not go on to get training for. Thus, he never made it big.

Imagine the conditioning our minds went through in such an environment, yet we wanted to make it big, because we saw other families who were living big and we knew big was possible. Hence, I grew up to become very introspective, and always looked at things rather differently from most people around me. I developed non-conformist ideas, because I wanted things to be different for me and my family.

At the time, all my dreams of what was possible were however being pivoted on middle class thinking without exposure, to creativity-enhancing education and experiences. Though, we had a better life than most families around us had, it was nonetheless a tough life.

Therefore, my life has consisted of a continuous desire to find my place of relevance and fulfillment, but life does not respond to need, it responds to desire, to faith, and to definite pursuits of predetermined goals. These goals can only be achieved utilizing definite plans in an environment of strong belief. These are the principles that I have had to learn and practice in the last eight years of my fourteen years in business, plus another seven years as an employee that have brought me to the point of writing this book to assist others like me on their journey.

There is a shift in the world order that we must all understand and appropriate to be able to navigate the world economy at this time for personal accomplishments and a greater global impact. There is a principle in the German culture called the 'zeitgeist'. This represents the general psyche prevalent at different periods of time amongst people and their belief system at such a time. It is also described as the spirit of the age. I bring this forth to buttress the point that the world is a dynamic system that evolves continually and responds at different time frames to different approaches to education, business, personal accomplishments, governance and everything else.

Our world has gone through the stone age, the agricultural age, the Industrial Age, and now we are in the information age. It is said now that information is power, though this is an incomplete statement. It is information that is applied that is power. That is a very crucial understanding you must hold on to as you read this book. Your readiness to apply the principles outlined in the pages of this book is the basic necessity for this book to make a true and lasting impact in your life. The commodity that our world craves above all else today is knowledge, or to put it in context, information. Countless numbers of the nouveau rich in today's world emerged based on transactions they engaged, in which they exchanged some new information for great wealth.

Information that is targeted at mind development and reprogramming is of vital importance today because the spirit of this age demands greater levels of accomplishments in virtually every field of endeavor. This demand can only be met by elevated thinking that will drive creativity and innovation, with the result being a much more advanced global space delivering better living standards, richer economies, and definitely, success and wealth.

In his low moments, my dad in blaming his 'misfortune' on Nigeria's economic quandary, used to tell us that his plan for his family was to have raised his children together with my mum in the United Kingdom. That was the fad for young educated Nigerians at the time. The country was on the verge of gaining independence from the United Kingdom and Nigerians got to travel to and live in Britain relatively easily. However, his plan was truncated by the death of his father and mother within months of each other in the late nineteen fifties. As the first son of his father, he had to stay back in Nigeria to help raise and educate his siblings by getting a job in the bank.

My dad blamed this turn of events for his not being able to give his children a better life, which he was convinced our holding British passports would guarantee. The sad reality inherent in this rather personal and emotional tale is that while my father was nursing his regrets on his 'misfortune', other fathers of his time were creating great wealth in the same Nigerian economy he was operating in. He was simply trapped by thought patterns that were inimical to success and wealth creation. Sadly, my dad had a mindset that worked against his very ambition in life to give his wife and children the best life possible. We lived a middle class life, which delivered to us quite a good dose of undesirable experiences.

We hear talk every day about the reduction of poverty across the world, wealth redistribution, and the narrowing of the gap between the rich and the poor. As desirable as these concepts are, we are not going to get any closer to making realities out of them if we continue to exercise the same methods that have been applied without success for decades. I think that comes very close to the definition of insanity.

## New Thinking

New thinking and approaches will be the resultant effect of mind shift. This starts with you the individual and permeates eventually into society as we continue to share this concept and its underlying principles. Gone are the days of traditional thinking cast in iron as it were. You must now embrace the new world order that requires you to get into the depths of your being and tap your inherent creative essence to bring the new you to light.

I recall the story of the two farmers, who in the early days of mechanized farming were faced with the option of utilizing new technology and machinery to improve their productivity. Mr. A, after taking some time to interact with the extension workers from the government chose to give the new approach a trial. Mr. B the other farmer would not even give the time to the officers to look at the information they had to share. He had heard rumors that the government was out to grab farmlands for new projects and as such, they intended to kill the soil of the farmlands to make it easier for farmers to abandon the lands. Moreover, he did not want to stop practicing farming the traditional, albeit spiritual, way his father had taught him, which he also learnt from his grandfather. The results of the two men and their decisions became obvious in just a short time frame. I will leave the details of their results to your imagination.

Nothing can be more self-defeating for anyone in today's world than for such a person to refuse to avail himself of the information needed to elevate his level of existence. The information required for success in any area of endeavor is out there, you just have to appropriate it. New thinking rules the world today. Call it thinking outside the box or new age thinking, it is, for all practical purposes, the same. You must learn to process information differently from now, if you are going to achieve new and greater success. An example of new thinking is as follows.

An elderly person or one who is advanced in years, traditionally will be described as being old. New thinking describes the same person as being aged. What is the point here? The term 'old' speaks of being obsolete or anachronistic, while 'aged' speaks of being experienced and possessing wisdom. Would you then rather be addressed as being past your time of relevance whilst you are still alive, or be described as possessing wisdom and experience needed in the present? More examples of new thinking as applied to issues of everyday life, like replacing 'handicapped' with 'physically challenged' and substituting 'insane' or 'crazy' with 'mentally challenged' make the psyche of today's world clearer.

New thinking, therefore, leads to new ideas which take creativity to new heights that will improve lives and deliver even more wealth creation and success. Like anything else of value and impact in life, new thinking has to be engaged deliberately by the person who intends to ride it as a vehicle to access a new life experience and reality.

# Chapter 2

## THE SYSTEM

"The established system prepares people to only
think in a certain pre-determined way."
**'Lolu Ogunmade**

Imagine the following scenario. A professor in the course
of teaching his students, to buttress a point says, 'one plus
one equals two'. One student with a searching look on his
face retorts, "where do I get the ones from before I can add
them up to arrive at two?" The professor with a confused
countenance answers, "I assume you must have gotten them
before coming to me to show you how to add them up".

This hypothetical scenario may seem somewhat simplistic
and probably even patronizing at the first read. The
divergence between conventional education and everyday
life realities, however, is what I intend to bring to you. We
operate in a system that is defective both, in its throughputs
and outputs, but which has been sustained through time and
is now solidly entrenched in society.

The hidden truth in this story is that professors and others who stay in classrooms to teach people how to be successful and to make money mostly do not know how to do so themselves, because they have not been exposed to the practical realities of being in the marketplace and turning a dollar into two. They possess mental acumen gathered from their own teachers which they have mostly not tested practically. Herein is the failure of today's educational system. It consists of curricula designed by the establishment to produce a set of people who have only been prepared to think in a certain way. They are called job seekers. They leave different schools with various certificates and proceed to look for jobs in businesses owned by the establishment.

They are not trained in the schools to engage with the creative essence they possess inherently to be creators of new directions and vistas needful for mankind's dominance of the earth to be furthered. Job seekers are human 'robots' that need conscious interruptions of their thought patterns to repair the damage that the educational system has inflicted on them. The failings of the educational systems of the world are quite difficult to see for most that are caught up in the system. This is because it is such a big system delivering so much profit to those who have invested in it at varying degrees. You can very easily get sucked into the routine that it becomes impossible to look at the system with the eye and mind of an outsider. All the while, the owners and patrons of the system get rich from the returns on their investments.

Has it ever crossed your mind that you leave school poorer than when you got in? It is true that you leave the school with a certain aggregation of facts and figures that makes you an expert in your particular area of study. When you

22

reduce it to dollars and cents however, you do leave the school poorer than when you got in! In most of the developed world people get student loans to go to college and are expected to pay back the loans when they start work. This means that by the time you leave the school system and start earning money based on your application of the knowledge acquired in school, or otherwise, you are already a debtor to the system!

In Nigeria where I come from, students are usually sponsored to school by parents and guardians who pay for the student's education in most instances. Therefore, in the same line of thought, all the money spent to educate the student supposedly can only and hopefully be gotten back from salaries and wages if the student eventually goes back to serve the system on a job.

The wealth that is lost to the system, in the context of this book, is not just in terms of the money paid to the schools, but the abuse that the mind and creative essence of the student would have been exposed to due to a prolonged interface with the system. The end product of the system, remember, is a job mentality expressed in different ways. Now, the system tells you that the information you gathered in school will pay you when you trade it within or outside the school. That is the pay off. Will you not rather engage with a system of learning and education that gives you the ability to create wealth, even while you learn?

However, this book is not written to condemn the established educational systems of the world, but to show the inherent limitations they create in the mind and its creative essence. My intent is to point the reader in a direction that encourages creativity in its limitless expression, despite having had some interface with the system. This is creativity that cannot be boxed into a collage of pre-determined outcomes by third parties. Little wonder that a good number of the people who have made the greatest impact on the world and in the history of mankind have been those who had relatively little contact, if any, with the system. Their minds retained the best part of the inherent creativity and they unleashed it to change the world! They are called Entrepreneurs.

These are the creative thinkers who choose, (who decide), to go forward by tapping into the innate creative essence to get their thoughts actualized. They stop at nothing! They engage with their thoughts and by utilizing definite plans and systems, they get the job done. These are the ones who have been intuitive enough to turn the tables back on the system to take from the system without being trapped in the system. These types of people are rare.

It is common knowledge that ninety-seven percent of the global work force is employed by the three per cent who own global business across all sectors. It takes a mindshift to move from the ninety seven to the three per cent category. Innovation and duplication of ideas, which form the bedrock of new business in the real world economy, are directly related to mind processes: thoughts and imaginations.

Some of the biggest corporations in the world today were products of simple, often silly or stupid sounding ideas (thoughts). Some of the feats recorded in history sounded like ideas borne of insanity when they were first muted, yet man put satellites in space, and went one step better when he orbited the earth and finally landed on the moon! An example of such a corporation is Ebay.

## The Ebay Story

In September 1995, Pierre Omidyar, born in Paris in 1967, launched a website called Auction Web to serve as a platform for online auctions. With a background in programming and having done some business with different partners and clients, he wanted to create a trading platform that he probably never thought would become what is now the Ebay of today.

Having sold an earlier company, eShop to Microsoft in 1991, Pierre was quite aware of the potential of e-commerce. Out of an effort to help his girlfriend at the time, who later became his wife, he created an area on his site for her to reach others within her area of interest. This led to the birth of Ebay as the volumes of traffic and transactions on his site increased at such a pace that made him create it as a full business platform. He started charging small fees for members on the site to put up their products and services.

This simple thought to solve a problem for his girlfriend became one of the most recognized e-commerce business platform of today, with virtually all kinds of items and services being traded on the many sites now operated by Ebay. It is estimated that twenty five million sellers list over eight hundred million items on ebay site, and are patronized by about one hundred and sixty two million users. This simple idea has now made Pierre Omidyar a global business leader, worth about eight billion dollars, leading a company with over eleven thousand employees and valued at about sixty billion dollars.

The hidden, yet plain truth in all of the countless achievements of man through the ages is that men can do anything they desire to do, so long as they are committed to the vision upon which the desire is founded. This principle is true in all the areas of human endeavor and enterprise.

## Working through the System

If you are the self development and entrepreneurial type who reads books and who uses other instructive materials on these subjects, you most likely would have been reminded at several times of the classical advice we all get from our parents. While growing up you must have been told to 'go to school, get good grades, so you can get a good job after school.'

This statement is probably the most poignant indicator of a mindset that is dominated by traditional ways of thinking. This pattern of thinking, which has been passed down through the ages, has now been identified in recent times as the strength on which the system thrives. As long as this is the predominant perspective among people, the system will always get its army of 'robots' to serve it. The boat will not be rocked. However, if we can get people to see the limitations that this mindset creates for the individual, maybe, just maybe, we can shift some minds.

People who have imbibed this notion have also imbibed a concept of life that makes them employees who get paid weekly or monthly salaries or wages for working for other people. While I will state categorically here that there is nothing wrong with you working for some other person if that is what you choose, I will ask you this question. 'Have you ever really thought about starting your own business and having others work for you? Think about it this way. This person or group of people that own the organization you currently work for have a vision and mission they are trying to accomplish. You do not determine the vision and mission, you are only engaged to assist to achieve them.

What this implies is that you spend your time through the most productive years of your life helping others to build their dreams and get paid whatever they decide is appropriate for the value you bring to their business. You leave off thinking about what you can start because you have found a comfort zone based on the mindset of getting a good job that you grew up with.

In most cases, people who work jobs cannot even identify what they are passionate enough about to build into a business for themselves. They are subject to the dictates of employers until they are deemed to be too old to continue working and they are then retired. This reminds me of the very popular term in the business and consulting world: the forty year sentence. You work forty hours a week for forty years and retire with forty percent of the pay that was not enough in the first place!

The point here is that you will not reach your full potential in life as long as you work for others. You can live a relatively good and comfortable life, but you definitely will not maximize your potential. Imagine what you would be doing if the organization you currently work for and all other employing businesses were not established by the founders. You will do something for yourself, even if it has to be by yourself alone. This is where your peculiar talents come to play.

27

There must be, and believe me, there is something unique to you that can become a value rendering venture to an identified market that can deliver great success to you. However, the system as is will not avail you the opportunity to discover yourself because it needs you to serve it. You must now use the information you are receiving through this book to liberate your mind, because you owe it to yourself.

Through the ages the system has reinvented and sustained itself by passing down the narrow-minded dogma to generations, so that children take over serving the system from their parents. Likewise, the children of the owners of the system take over the reins of control from their parents and become the bosses of the children of the retired employees. This is the vicious life cycle that the system offers. The proprietors of the system make things happen by getting the servants of the system to work to get things done. The good thing is that you now have a choice as to which side of the divide you want to operate from.

## Mastering the System
Mastering the system, simply put, is the ability to take enough experience and expertise from the system and to use these in collaboration with other parameters as assets to exploit the same system for personal achievement and freedom.

This sounds somewhat technical, but the break down is simple. Most people will transit into being entrepreneurs from working jobs, public service, (including military and paramilitary institutions) and volunteering in charities.

All of these institutions comprise the established system dominating world affairs, and all of these organizations offer some form of training or another to people who serve in them. The average person can therefore get some basic idea of how organizations are built and run and even some training on finance and investment, which such a person can take away from having been in the system.

This basic exposure to the operations of organizations can thus become an asset that can be improved upon as it is combined with the peculiar talents, desire and strategy by anyone who is so disposed. You will find that a great number of today's celebrated entrepreneurs have failed repeatedly in different businesses that they started as they learned the ropes of business. Their persistent pursuit of their dreams combined with education in various forms, mentoring relationships, and belief however eventually made the icons out of them that we celebrate today. They are examples of people who have mastered the system.

You should therefore not be afraid to fail a few times before you succeed. You will be in good company through the process, because even the great icons of today's business world still fail in some of the ventures they engage, even now. The pay off here is that when you become a master of the system, the door is opened to you to play with the 'big boys' who own and control the system. You are said to have arrived.

# Chapter 3

## THOUGHTS AND IMAGINATIONS

"As a man is thinking, so he is becoming....
thinking is a continuum."
**'Lolu Ogunmade**

The mind is the singular, most powerful part of a person in relation to life outcomes. Mankind has power over the earth basically due to our ability to think, to rationalize, or to be logical. Other living creatures are subject to man because they lack the ability to think. In spite of the fact that there are so many animals that are bigger and stronger than man, they are all subject to man. Definitely, there is some level of primitive intelligence that can be associated with the lives of some creatures, but they obviously do not operate at the level of thought particular to humans.

Thoughts and imaginations are domiciled in the mind. The mind therefore can be seen as a store that receives and keeps information coming as thoughts and imaginations. The information in the mind is stored as images, which is why thoughts are received by a person as images and not as a stream of words in a sentence or several sentences. For instance, if you were to think of your favorite dog breed right now, what you see in your mind will not be the letters that form the name of that dog breed, but a picture or an image of the dog. Therefore, a thought impulse brings an image to the consciousness of a person, but the process of ruminating on the image to arrive at a certain conclusion or course of action is thinking.

In similar manner, imagination is the stringing together of several and diverse images in the mind deliberately. While thinking can be both active and passive, imagination is deliberate and active.

The point behind my going into the foregoing explanation on thoughts and imaginations is simple. The mind holds in it all the information, (knowledge) that makes a person who he or she is. The power such a person will wield in any area of life will be dependent on the information stored up in that mind. The thinking patterns of the person will also be dictated by the 'contents' of that mind and most importantly, the attitudes of the person to life in all aspects will flow from the same mind. This is because attitudes have been described as a collection of thoughts in the mind of a person that have become so powerful that they dictate the life pattern of the person. The way the person sees the world around him and his response to it is dependent on the thoughts that have been stored in his mind about the world.

We can only draw from what we have in store. Therefore, your mind renders to you the basic ingredients that inspire and control your thinking and imagination. The good book of scriptures says, "as a man thinks in his heart (mind), so is he." You become what you think about! You become what you imagine!

An extended meaning of the same verse of scripture is this, as a man is thinking, so he is becoming. This is easy to comprehend once you recognize that thinking is a continuous exercise that people engage in all day long, every day, either actively or passively. Even when the actual thought at any particular point is of no obvious creative nature and value, it remains a thought, albeit suggested from external sources and adds to the overall mindset of the individual. You are either thinking for yourself or thoughts are being thrown at you by the world around you on an on-going basis. This, therefore, adds to the continuing transformation that you as a person are going through.

In essence, the mind is the production line on which the person you see today was produced. The deeper realization is that this production line never stops working as it keeps updating its production with information received. What this brings to the fore is the fact that as a person, you are entrenched in your perspective, thinking, and attitudes as you fill your mind with even more information.

## Mind Conditioning

What has become the way of the world, with regards to the upbringing we all are exposed to, is more negative inputs into the mind than positive. It has been said countless times and written in so many books and studies that the average child hears a disproportionate count of 'no' as compared to 'yes' in the formative years. Parents and other adults say more of 'you can't do that', 'stop that' and 'don't go there' to children than more affirmative things like 'you can do it', go for it!' and 'yes you can'.

This predisposition in parents and guardians results in the mind of the growing child being caged as it were. The child becomes more aware of limiting factors than motivating success. A person brought up in such an environment learns instinctively to search for reasons why things cannot be done in almost every aspect of life. The mindset of this person is defective, and this is a result of the environment and information ingrained in the mind.

As a father of a set of twins, who are now just over four years old, a girl and a boy, I am well aware of the fine line between a good and disciplined upbringing and a restrained mind. I still struggle to find a good balance, but I am committed to exposing my children to everything that will expand their thinking and mind. I must at the same time communicate to my children the sense of responsibility and discipline that will make them assets to the larger society rather than the opposite. We must not fall into the trap of leaving children who are yet to come to the age of accountability and responsibility to start making decisions about life under the pretext of allowing them to freely express their individualities.

My oldest nephew asked me a question over ten years ago. *"Uncle 'Lolu"*, he said, *"when chickens grow up, do they become turkeys?"* My first reaction was a sense of amazement that made me start laughing, but I saw that sincerity akin to children in his eyes, and I answered by explaining to him that chickens and turkeys though similar, are actually two different types of birds. What struck me as I thought about his question some more was the boy's ability to look at both animals to recognize the similarities between them in detail enough to project that the smaller one of the two could grow to become the 'larger version' in time. His young mind had created a time line of the life of the chicken and had arrived at the conclusion that the turkey could only have started as a chicken! What great imagination the young lad possesses. That is amazing.

## Right Thinking

The realization that you become what you think puts a responsibility on you to think the right thoughts, if you are going to positively impact the world, and if you are going to live a successful life; because thoughts are powerful and carry positive or negative energy with them. Thoughts are alive.

Psychologists and other scientific disciplines readily talk about the energy of thoughts from the view points of quantum physics, direction, and speed. This means that the energy of thoughts can be measured, while thoughts can be directed in specific terms, and can be transmitted through space and time. While my intent is not to get overly scientific, I need to bring these facts about the power of thoughts to you to get you to see the importance of learning to think right.

## Right Thinking and Positive Thinking

Right thinking goes beyond the popular concept of positive thinking. This is simply because an individual may maintain a posture of positive thinking about what he aims to achieve, yet have a motive that is much less than honorable for pursuing his goal. Right thinking therefore, as subjective as it may be construed, speaks more to the overall personality and world view of the individual. It is rather idealistic, but puts the person in a position to look beyond self in his life pursuits. He learns to view himself as part of a great collective and as such integrates his desires into the bigger picture. What this results in is the reinforcement of the humanity of the individual. We learn to be more tolerant, accommodating and more compassionate. We learn to be at peace with others and with our own selves.

Right thinking will make us weigh our actions more critically before we execute them. As leaders in the workplace, social groups, family and government, we will be able to appreciate the effects of our decisions on people. The majority of the crises across the world today will cease to exist if only some right thinking was adopted by the dramatis personae. Selfishness, which is in direct contrast with right thinking, is the order of the day now. It is pulling the world into an abyss, yet it is gaining grounds as people refuse to recognize the need for a mindshift in this regard.

The desire for individual success in isolation of the consideration of all other areas of impact, as opposed to seeking the collective good, is an aberration that is the underlying problem of these times. The point I am making is not that to seek personal success is wrong, but that we must learn to pursue our ambitions with a mindset that is global in outlook.

## The Conscious and Subconscious Mind

The mind is divided into the two parts generally referred to as the conscious and subconscious minds. The conscious part of the mind functions primarily based on the impulses it receives from the natural senses: sight, taste, touch, hearing, and smell. The conscious mind interprets information received through the senses and sends action commands to the body based on its interpretations.

The subconscious mind on the other hand is the seat of character formation. This is because mind information is stored in the subconscious and processed in thoughts. This, of course, leads to the formation of attitudes and mindsets, which reflect the world view of the person. The subconscious though passive and completely dispassionate in its essence, is always alert and ready to receive information. This is why it is said that the subconscious mind never goes to sleep even when the conscious mind does.

Personality and character are formed in the subconscious mind, and acted out through the conscious mind. An understanding of this is very important as it will buttress the need for you to ensure that only the right kind of information is exposed to your mind in every aspect of life. Repeated and continuous exposure to negative information and images will only produce negative attitudes and results in the life of a person. The opposite will be the result in the life of that person who ensures that only positive information is stored up in the mind.

## Short Circuiting the Negative

We live in communities and as such images, information,

36

and even impulses will come to us from external sources on a daily basis. Hence, it is a challenge to always live in an atmosphere of uninterrupted positives. You must learn to short circuit the negatives that will be thrown at you before they are ingrained in your subconscious. You must.

Most electrical appliances have fuses in them that cause them to short circuit, or to cut off a sudden surge in the flow of electricity through that appliance to avoid a mishap. The point here is that you have to build a 'fuse' into your consciousness that helps you to quickly recognize a negative impulse coming at you and to immediately cut off from that flow. A practical example of this is mastering how to immediately change the topic when a negative person throws bad information into a conversation with you. It may even be an action step, like moving away from such a negative person to cut off the conversation.

I may not be able to control what you have stored in your mind, but I sure can stop you from dumping your negatives on me. I owe that to myself. A mistake that is common is that out of a desire to be polite or nice, people stay in environments that are inimical to positive mind outcomes. You may find it necessary, as you engage your transformative process, to cut off some relationships, or at the least limit the time you spend with some folks. Be bold to take the necessary action.

## Tap the Power of Imagination
I said earlier that imagination is a deliberate action in its very nature. There is so much power that an active imagination

can generate for you if you learn to tap into this creative resource. The simple reason is this: while actually going on that desirable six week vacation to the Carribean Islands could cost an arm and a leg, imagining yourself and your significant other already on the white sandy beaches enjoying the cool breeze will cost you absolutely nothing. It is as simple as thinking about it and connecting with the thought emotionally. The full impact of this power is experienced when you hold on to your imagination to the point where the pictures are engraved in your subconscious mind. Your subconscious mind will digest the images up to the point where it will get your conscious mind to buy into the possibilities and you will see a series of events take place that will bring you to the physical experience desired.

The negativity in popular culture today ridicules people with vivid imaginations as pipe dreamers who are not expected to achieve or amount to much. Have you ever told someone in some kind of relationship with you what you expect from life and that person laughs at you? Let me surprise you by announcing to you that you need to re-envision that desire, if it is something you really believed to be possible at any time. If your dreams are not literally stupendous, both to you and your audience, they probably are not big enough dreams to be worth your time.

What do you imagine Sir Richard Branson and Elon Musk got as responses from the first set of people they told they wanted to commercialize space travel for the adventuring rich person? Although I was not in those meetings, I dare say that they most likely did not get very encouraging answers from those people. Today however, both men are so close to achieving their dreams of human and other aspects of space travel that they must have pushed the frontiers backwards now.

I have a mind image right now of this book, Mindshift, on the shelves of the best bookstores around the world in more countries and translated into more languages than I am aware are in existence. I see the e-books, the audio books and the spin offs from this work! That is why I have committed to writing the book and to going through the journey of getting it published, though I have never been down this road before. It is not about success for me, though that cannot be avoided, it is about proving the principles outlined in the book to be true. It is about giving to the universe what it demands of me at this time, what it delivered to me at the first. If you imagine a thing and hold on to it as passionately as any desire can be held on to, it is just a matter of time till it becomes an existential reality.

*Chapter 4*

# INHIBITORS TO MINDSHIFT

"A closed mind to superior knowledge is a closed door to growth and success."
**'Lolu Ogunmade**

As desirable as the thought of turning out with a reconditioned mind that attracts the success that we desire can be, there are yet thought based inhibiting factors to experiencing a mindshift. The experience of a mindshift will definitely come to each individual at some point in life where he or she already has an established lifestyle. This lifestyle is based on attitudes, which are formed from thinking patterns peculiar to the individual. These collections of thoughts that mark the individuality of each person may present any of the following inhibitors to mindshift.

## Perception
The life of an individual will be very deeply impacted by how such a person sees the world. I am not referring here to just looking at the visible physical world, but to the

interpretation the individual gives to what is observed by the eyes. Perception is the totality of the mental and sensual digestion and subsequent interpretation of the world by a person. In this context, the world represents people, places and events or experiences. Perception is a mind function that is so powerful, because it affects the way an individual reads the world. Hence, by extension, affects the way the person responds to the world.

It represents the individual's attitude to the world, which is the result of the sum total of how the person thinks about the world. This is why a glass can be filled to half its height with water, and two people are told to describe it: one will likely say the glass is half full, while the other will say the glass is half empty. That is perception; two world views of the very same issue, situation or event. By definition and extension, we may view the two descriptions as being optimistic and being pessimistic. Perception is what makes people suspicious, withdrawn, afraid, lonely, happy, joyful, courageous, grateful and adventurous. It is like the two sides of a coin. The sad reality is that most people hold a pessimistic view of life and this limits them to a miserable and mediocre life. Their perception is continuously negative and this is one of the most powerful inhibitors to mindshift.

## Unbelief

This is another major inhibitor to mindshift. It is quite disheartening to acknowledge that the scourge of unbelief is rampant across various demographics. I have been in business opportunity sessions where I share information with a set of opportunity seekers and I can see just by looking into people's eyes that they do not believe what I am saying to them.

I remember a particular lady who was in one of such sessions that I facilitated in the second quarter of last year. I had gotten to the point in my presentation where I was showing the class the different levels of the cash payments in the compensation plan of an organization I partner with when the lady exclaimed in unbelief.

I turned to look at her and I said, 'you don't believe me madam. You don't believe a company can pay so much to anyone'. She looked rather embarrassed, but nodded to confirm that she did not believe what I was saying. Recognizing her embarrassment, I turned to the class and took a few minutes to address the unbelief I knew was definitely in some of the other minds in the room before I went back to the compensation plan.

The sad truth is that a lot of folks out there have tried and tried through time to make things work, to reach their goals and to be able to live in prosperity and they have failed, sometimes severally. In defeat they have convinced themselves that success is not achievable. They have not learnt how to fail forward. Thus, they cannot trust any promise of success, no matter what platform it is being presented upon. Some, probably most of these people, have developed a mental defense mechanism that kicks in whenever a promise of success, opportunity or even prosperity is encountered. This negative instinct kicks in and tells them not to trust or believe the promise. 'After all, success is not for folk like me', they tell themselves.

A mind that is closed to new information due to unbelief cannot experience a mindshift, and such a person will be relegated to the realm of mediocrity. In truth very little can be achieved with such an individual.

## An Unforgiving Mindset

You may be burdened with an unforgiving mental state which may be directed at yourself or some other person due to some event or experience from your past. This mental state also constitutes a major impediment to mindshift, because not being able to forgive yourself or a third party leaves your life basically in limbo.

The energy expended on the inability to let go of some feeling of failure, hurt, and even underperformance in your past engenders does absolutely nothing to help you. You must get this right at this instant. Just like guilt that is not overcome, an unforgiving mindset weighs you down so much that you are completely drained of any desire to aspire for any experience that will engender a mindshift. It creates a wall around you that breeds suspicion, antagonism, and even a reclusive propensity.

Life and people are not perfect, just as much as you are not perfect. You must let go of that memory file that holds in it the negative experience and its accompanying negative emotion. You must learn to completely delete that memory from your mind so you can forgive. Forgive yourself and forgive whoever has scarred your mind. You need to, if you must progress on the journey to your new self that life and living is all about.

43

Failure, hurt, underperformance on some obligation and any other demerit that may engender guilt and an unforgiving mindset must be put in perspective as part of the process of growth and maturity. Mistakes will be made and hopefully corrected, bad choices, associations and investments will be made too. However, you should not let these learning experiences become anything other than what they are, learning experiences.

## The Perfectionist Disposition

The 'everything must be just right before ...' or 'I must have it all together before ...' mentality serves as yet another major setback to experiencing a mindshift. The truth about life is simple, and this truth is that never will a time come when everyone and everything will be perfectly aligned with your desires or pursuits. The pursuit of perfection in any and every human endeavor, therefore, is the pursuit of an elusive phantom.

The desire or demand that an ideal environment be created or that the information and images that will spur a mindshift be delivered in a specific way will only result in the overall self denial of this great experience.

This is a conclusion that I have arrived at based on my own experience. I grew up as the son of a banker in the early seventies. Though my dad left banking right at the end of the seventies decade, he left the industry with a character that was quite particular about stuff. He was very fussy about some things, and if you had to do a chore in the home you had better go at it the way dad showed you to do it. This of course meant that we did not see eye to eye on a number of issues in my earlier years, to put it lightly.

The result of this was that by the time I was in high school, I had developed perfectionist tendencies that became entrenched deep in my mind. Things just had to be in a certain arrangement in the house for me to be comfortable. My clothes have to be ironed so smoothly that I would not see any wrinkle. A glass of water had to be filled to an exact invisible mark, and a bunch of other things that I insisted on. This tendency also affected my friendships with regards to what I expected of my friends, though I always managed to avoid rubbing off on them badly enough to lose their friendship.

As I grew and matured I could see how the perfectionist in me was making life rather difficult for the people closest to me and really, for me too. Though, I still have a good deal of the tendency in me, I have learnt to devolve it in productive areas. I have learnt to be easy to a large extent and to allow for the imperfections of life and people, because I see my own imperfections first. I have become more tolerant and appreciative of the fact that perfection is an objective and not an obligation.

The need to take things easy minute by minute, hour by hour and day by day is also the need to give room for improvement and not to focus on what is not in sync with our grand picture. Life's beauty is wrapped in all of its imperfections, and our ability to navigate through these challenges adds color to living.

## The Victim Disposition

This inhibitor to mindshift shows up in various ways. I will point out a few of its types.

## The Class or Status Victim

People with this mindset see themselves as victims of the societies in which they exist from the angle of coming from a lower class caste, ethnic group, or a less prominent race. Others within the same caste or race see themselves as being from the bottom rungs of the status ladder. They are therefore resigned to believing that 'the good life' is not for them and they will actually sabotage any attempt to get them to view life differently.

My corporate and consumer goods supply business takes me to India at times, where I source my products from. India culturally has a caste system in which the darker a person's skin tone is, the lower the caste they belong to. Also, the part of the country a person comes from may be a factor. This automatically means that such lower caste Indians are denied opportunities to get ahead in any sphere of life. They are more likely even to be deprived of the amenities the state should ordinarily make available to all citizens.

With globalization and modernization now becoming the trend, the governments at different levels are fighting to change these cultural practices that go against internationally accepted standards. These attempts are yet being met with strong resistance, and some good portion of resistance is from the sufferers of the caste system themselves. They don't believe they deserve better and that their lives can be lived at the same quality as those of the so called higher castes. They have imbibed the victim mindset.

In Nigeria the caste system also exists in some cultures within our multi-ethnic nation. This aberration that people and societies inflict on other people has through generations led to keeping billions of people in miserable and mediocre levels of existence.

## The Education Victim

These are the set of people who blame their lack of proper education, at whatever level, for the realities they are confronted with. They believe they are way past the age of getting an education and as such, they deserve to be stationed where life and society has left them. This mindset they hold on to, despite knowing that various forms of late and adult education systems are available to them.

They will give countless reasons why they are not suitable for the available adult education systems and why vocational training will not work for them. Some even have religious reasons for not getting an education, yet they blame not having an education for the rut they live in. It is something like a catch twenty two – 'I cannot get educated because my religion forbids conventional or western education, and I cannot move up in life because I am not educated!'

It is necessary to emphasize that education in the context of this book is not the school systems and curricular available out there, but the exposure of the mind in time to information in an environment that will inspire a mindshift.

47

Paraphrasing Napoleon Hill from his all time best-selling book, THINK AND GROW RICH: "he is not educated who possesses a set of generalized or specialized information gathered from some school(s) over a period of time. He is educated who by developing his mind, knows how to get out of life what he wants without infringing on the rights of another."

## The Poverty Victim

This is simply a disposition towards blaming one's family background and history of lack or poverty for the present state of nothingness. This individual has found a comfort zone in looking back at his pedigree and seeing the generations before him that made no meaningful impact on their community. He therefore believes that he cannot be any different from his forebears and sees no need to even aspire to any lofty idea or ideal.

Quite similar in comparison with the status victim, the poverty victim resigns to fate while holding on to the belief that his type of people only exist to serve the privileged. He is therefore living with a deep sense of resentment towards himself and the world around him. He is quick to accuse the rich as people who have robbed society based on their privileged positions. To this person rich or wealthy people are 'sinners', more or less. His mind has been shut down and he only exists in limbo. He may even possess an entitlement mindset, which tells him that society owes him the comforts of life even as he maintains an unwillingness to venture.

This is a sad reality that is common across the world, even in the developed countries. The gap between the poor and the rich is said to be fast widening, and there seems to be little or nothing that can be done to reverse the trend.

## The Health Victim

It is an established fact that a great portion of the population of the world today are dealing with myriads of health challenges. Chronic diseases and debilitating conditions are on the rise. The health victim is either blaming the particular health challenge confronting him for his inability to pursue any life goal, or he is waiting to be cured before he starts anything seriously engaging.

He cannot see or understand that in many instances, the adoption of a life achievement goal has been the trigger for the recovery of a lot of people from quite serious conditions. It may even be something as little as picking up a new habit or sports activity that can go with a person's health challenge that becomes the trigger.

The world is full of stories of people who despite very serious health issues have changed the course of the world in practically every aspect of life. People who are physically challenged have become leaders of nations, sports, entertainment icons, and business leaders of the highest quality. Some, despite suffering from seriously debilitating illnesses have gone ahead to champion finding cures and better treatment options for those same illnesses and diseases. The health victim, however, will explain all the facts of the achievements of challenged people like him away, and yet produce reasons why he cannot do likewise.

Though other inhibitors to mindshift can be discussed here, they are basically spin-offs of these major ones that have been outlined.

A closed mind in any respect that fails to acknowledge and embrace superior knowledge will not get anyone any bit closer to living a life of impact and fulfillment. There is always an opportunity for growth, but these opportunities are tied to mind reconditioning and development. Mind development, and ultimately mindshift, are functions of a new body of information or knowledge that a person embraces. I guess this is why it is said that life is a process of learning that never ends

## The Other Picture

The quest for a more fulfilling life both in the quality of our lives and the impact we have on the larger society often demands that we overcome the dictates of our preconditioned minds. You must learn to unlearn, and to welcome new perspectives and experiences to bring about the opportunities that come with new thinking made possible by new knowledge.

I have a friend who happens to be one of my best friends ever, who recently shared with me how he arrived at the decision to marry his wife. He told me how and why he waited for a considerably longer period of time than is usual in these parts to settle down into a married life. As it is common to most, he had a clear picture of what he wanted his future wife to look like, her height and skin color, her nationality, everything was clearly spelt out.

My buddy shared with me how that every lady he met in his search for the love of his life that came close to his picture seemed to have some issue or another that made it impossible for him to establish a lifelong relationship with her. The chemistry was not just right, and he always ended up discontinuing each relationship. The years went by and he kept trying to find that lady who would meet the set criteria perfectly, but she never showed up. Then finally, just by chance, he meets this lady who was completely out of his picture through a friend. He never even saw her as a potential 'Miss right' because she did not look anything like he wanted in his woman.

However, a second meeting with this lady left him with some inkling that she could be the one he had been searching for. He immediately pushed the thought out of his mind. Friends and common interests kept bringing both of them into close proximity repeatedly, and the questions on his mind concerning her being the one for him increased. They became friends and he eventually decided to ask her out just to get a chance to check her out beyond the external 'demerits'. He discovered a woman like none other from his history and the decision to ask her to be his wife became easy to make.

My friend had to disregard the image and information he had stored in his mind with regards to his choice of a wife, to move from bachelorhood to being happily married to the woman he now describes as the love of his life.

I could have pushed the argument that he settled for less than he wanted since the principles of desire and passion, among others outlined in this book, are known to guarantee the manifestation of the object of desire eventually. However, my friend realized that he had all along put the wrong criteria out there in identifying the woman for him. Though he met several ladies who met the criteria outwardly, they were inwardly not right for him. The moment he reached this understanding, (the moment when his mindshift was complete), he was able to recognize another woman who met his approval, though she does not look anything like his old criteria.

A closed mind that rejects superior information never benefits anyone. Such a state of being will only result in stagnation and mediocrity.

# Chapter 5

## MINDSHIFT

"Experiencing a mindshift can be like swimming against the current..."

**'Lolu Ogunmade**

We all come into this life and world with a mind that is much more like a blank slate than anything else. The mind is like a book with inexhaustible pages, which once opened, starts collecting information and images that it processes on an on-going basis throughout an individual's life. Information processing goes on simultaneously in the two parts of the mind. These are the conscious mind and the subconscious mind. Images and information pass from the conscious to the subconscious mind continuously.

The processing of the received information results in the character and perception of the individual. This processing of information is unique to each individual. There are no two persons that ever lived or are alive, that are exact replicas of one another. This is true for even the most similar set of identical twins. I dare say that even cloning cannot bring forth two identical persons with exact same personalities, perceptions and mindsets. This is simply because each individual processes information differently, even when the difference between them is minute.

The truth that children inherit certain traits from their parents and other characteristics peculiar to a family, clan, or even a tribe does not lead to the emergence of the exact same mindset, attitudes and world view among the persons in such a collective. There will always be divergent traits found in some individual(s) in a collection of people, no matter how closely related they are. It is like saying that there are always exceptions to a rule. Everyone born into this world is unique.

There is an innate factor in every individual that guides the processing of the images and information stored in the mind that leads to the formation of that person's personality. A mindshift affects this very factor to bring about a resultant change in mindset, perception and attitudes of the individual. The changes may be subtle or quite drastic, based on variables, which trigger such changes, like lack, desire, environment and associations.

Experiencing a mindshift can be as forceful as a ship getting swept in an opposite direction by gale force winds and it can also be as peaceful as floating in a pool on a floater. The experience is however not as important as the result. This is because the rest of the life of the individual going through a mindshift will be defined by the changes in different aspects of life that come with the experience. It either happens or it doesn't.

Going through a mindshift can be like swimming against the current in a river. The mind of the individual is confronted by information that runs at cross purposes with the status quo. The choice to embrace and engage with the new and to reject the status quo results in a mindshift. This choice for or against the status quo always has to be made. And this choice is really made in the subconscious mind.

The subconscious mind is the strongest part of the mind, because it is the reservoir of all received images and information where traits like perception, attitudes and character are formed based on the processing of images and information. The conscious mind is less powerful because it is dependent on the senses of taste, touch, smell, sight and sound. It is therefore sensory in its functioning, which presents a limitation, whereas the subconscious mind relies on subliminal impulses in its functioning. The conscious mind is subjective in nature because of its dependence on the five senses, whilst the subconscious mind is rather objective in function as it only receives and interprets images sent to it through the conscious mind.

This is why a mindshift will only take place in the subconscious mind and be transmitted to the conscious mind, which gives expression to the mindshift. The conscious mind feeds the subconscious with the information that ultimately results in a mindshift. The mindshift is then communicated to the conscious mind through which the changes that have occurred in the individual in perception, thinking, attitudes, and even character, due to the mindshift, are lived out or expressed.

## Mind Shift and Mindset

It is important to outline the relationship between mindset and mindshift to bring out the point of view this book communicates. A mindset is arrived at as a person digests images and information through time. The way a person processes the received information leads to the formulation of the mindset and world view of the individual. This can also be stretched to encompass the mindset of communities developed and passed down to generations through oral traditions and other cultural practices peculiar to a society. A mindset therefore denotes definiteness of personality. It speaks of structure and/or rigidity.

A mindshift on the other hand, speaks of a movement or displacement of the mindset based on the impact of a new body of information that counters what has been stored up in the mind of an individual or community to bring forth a new world view, perception, and ultimately, a new mindset. This results in new attitudes and personality changes that are observable.

## Renewing Your Mind

The good book of scriptures urges people to renew their minds to be able to live fulfilled lives that will be pleasing to God. The concept of renewing the mind denotes a renovation of the mind. This suggests therefore, an action of tearing down and moving things stored up in the mind, either to some back corner or a complete removal of those identified things from the mind.

This also ties up perfectly with the scripture that tells us that as a man is thinking so he is becoming. Renovating the mind, thus, implies cleaning out old thinking patterns, which have resulted in the attitudes and character of the individual to make room for a fresh body of thoughts that will result in a new man. This fresh body of thoughts will only come from exposure to a new set of images and information. You require new learning, new thinking, new friendships, new social circles, and other such exposures and experiences that will impact positively on the mind.

Therefore, a mindshift is a definite and recognizable experience when it happens to a person. You may not at the onset of your mindshift realize what is going on, but it becomes noticeable both to you and others in time.

All the wrong inputs that have been stored in your subconscious mind particularly, which make you function way below your true potential must be jettisoned. You must make a deliberate decision to reinforce mindshift by feeding your subconscious mind the right images and information. These become the bedrock of your mind functions, as your subconscious ingrains the new material on your conscious mind. Thus, it is said that what you read, the audios you listen to, the videos you watch, and the people you associate with will determine the contents of your subconscious that make or mar you as an individual.

One of the earliest signals to me that a shift was taking place in my mind as I think back now, was my learning to deliberately see things through the eyes of other people and to thereby avoid strife and conflict in most circumstances. I realized that most conflicts are engendered by the failure of people to view an issue from the point of view of another. Thus, because everyone only fixes their mind on how they supposedly have been wronged, taken for granted, or cheated, without trying to understand the other person's perspective of the same situation, crisis situations get worsened. This results in damage being done to great and beautiful relationships, whether they are families, marriages, corporate conflicts, and even conflicts between nations.

## My High School Fight

In 1985, I was in my third year of high school and was the class captain. I had an argument with a boy from another class who, like me, was also in his third year. It almost degenerated into a fist fight, but we stopped at telling each other that we would settle the scores after school behind our block of classrooms. I did not really expect anything to happen after school other than both of us going to our different homes.

The other boy must have been reminded by others that we 'had a date' after school, because he actually walked up to me to pick things up from where we left off. I was cornered! The whole group that was there earlier had gathered around the two of us prodding us to fight each other. To walk away, was all I really wanted to do, but that would have labeled me 'a weak mummy's boy' and I could not bear such a label. Hence, we went behind the block of classrooms as planned, with a crowd around us, and we got into a tussle. At a point, I hit him on his lips and he retaliated by hitting me across the face. I noticed he had blood in his mouth and at the same time I thought about the possibility of getting my eyes hurt if we continued, because the boys around us were mounting pressure on us to get nasty with each other.

Suddenly I dropped my fists and told him we needed to stop before we hurt each other badly and get into trouble with the school authorities. He saw reason with me, and we walked away from each other with each fighter having his group of 'supporters' assuring him that he was the better of the two. That's the kind of damage peer pressure can do to a misguided young person! That was the last physical fight I ever got into.

I particularly demonstrated to myself by putting a stop to the fight that I was indeed becoming a different young man than my environment encouraged. I was imbibing a different set of thought impulses and that was bringing forth a different perspective to conflicts and disagreements in me. I have held on to the same mindset till today.

As I grew older, I consciously started asking myself questions on why someone who I felt had done me some wrong would take such an action before I got confrontational with the person as I was wont to in time past. This always calmed me down. I ended up with much less quarrelling in my life and learnt to just let people be while protecting myself as much as I saw needful. While holding on to the principles upon which my life is built, I took responsibility for not getting readily upset by people and circumstances and found it much easier to relate with people of different personalities and temperaments.

A clear proof of this transformation in my mind to me is the fact that people still ask me today how I cope with and manage relating with certain people that most others around me avoid contact with. I guess I should say, on the lighter side, that I am still learning how to operate like this with my wife. Is that an 'exception to the rule?'

The importance of this to anyone experiencing a mindshift is that the observations that the people around express serve to assure the person that the changes occurring are real and recognized. The fact that people see and acknowledge the changes in the person reaffirms to the person that something positive has begun, which should be allowed to proceed to its end point.

Think of a person who you have always known to be the negative voice in any gathering with your friends, who suddenly comes forward with a word of appreciation to you for some favor. You probably will not pay much attention to him, because his remarks are out of character. However, when this friend makes a highly crucial suggestion on an issue that he most likely would have derided in his usual mode, you take cognizance that something is not quite the same with this friend of yours. You start to observe him more closely and the next time he shows this new positive disposition you most likely will ask him for an explanation as to what is going on with him.

The exchange between both of you when he attempts to give an answer to you will bring to his realization that something commendable is going on with him. This positive affirmation from you and others will only result in a resolve to stay on the right path.

The power of a positive affirmation in any aspect of life cannot be overemphasized. Positive energy can only birth even more positive energy, which when invested in any pursuit or quest delivers better results. This is also why a mindshift will only have positive results when it is incubated in a positive environment. On the converse, a negative environment will produce the reverse. The consequences of a negative mindshift may include various forms of undesirable anti-social and psychopathic behavioral patterns.

I remember a story we were told repeatedly as children, as part of the many things parents and guardians used to instill morals in us. I cannot tell if it really happened or not. It was said that a young man who had become an armed robber in Nigeria's early days of independence was eventually caught, prosecuted and sentenced to death by firing squad. We were told that as he stood tied to the stake to be shot he was asked to make a last request.

He reportedly asked that his mother be given a chance to come to him so he could speak with her for the last time. His request was granted, and when she came to him, he asked her to come close so he could whisper in her ear. He bit his mother's ear so badly that she bled profusely! When asked why he bit her, he reportedly said she was responsible for his being convicted. He went on to say that when he started petty stealing as a little boy, his mother encouraged him. She was excited at the things he was bringing home and prodded him to get more. Therefore, he grew to become the armed robber who was now tied to a stake awaiting the bullets that would kill him, because of the environment his mother created around him.

Negative energy breeds negative mind dispositions, and negative images and information result in a negative mindshift. You cannot totally prevent negative thoughts, images and information being thrown at you in the world we live in, but you can and must learn to filter what goes beyond your external senses and into your subconscious mind.

## MindShift and Paradigm Shift

While a mindshift is the result of a substitution of the dominating thoughts in the subconscious; a paradigm shift on the other hand is the end point of the process. This is because a paradigm shift is the noticeable displacement of the structured or molded pattern of thinking in an individual. A mindshift helps to unravel and dislodge the non-supportive information in the mind of the person in the context of the emergence of the true essence of the person by ingraining new information in the mind.

This distinction between mindshift and paradigm shift is important, because it is easy to view the former as simply a pseudonym for the latter. That conclusion, however, will be completely wrong. The man or woman you see in your mirror lives out the reality of what the mind is made up of. Remember that as a man is thinking so he is becoming. A mindshift therefore targets the stored information in your mind to get you to a point where you embrace new information. This brings about new thought patterns in you, which consequently birth a new set of attitudes that are, in substance, an aggregate of particular thoughts that then determine your mindset.

The new mindset arrived at is the new paradigm. A paradigm shift is thus, a product of a mindshift, whether it is recognized or not by the person going through the process. I should bring to your notice at this point that life does not stop to allow for our ignorance in any area or aspect of existence. Life flows by and we are faced with a choice to catch up, or be left in oblivion.

These two principles are therefore mutually supportive, as they are steps or markers in the process of the emergence of a new man. They are very crucial steps in the quest to discover and harness the creative essence of a person and to maximize the inherent potentials.

# Chapter 6

## FIND YOUR PASSION

"Your goal is your destination; Passion is the fire,
the energy that keeps your engine running"
**'Lolu Ogunmade**

Passion is the fire, the energy that drives a person in the direction of exploiting the talents and skills he possesses to attain fulfillment. It is the energy that we ride on to accomplish any given task. Passion cannot be missing in any meaningful life pursuit and accomplishment.

Everyone has something at some point in time that they are passionate about. In the context of human achievement, it is often said that what a person is most passionate about is probably a pointer to what that person's occupation or vocation should be. This is because the passion that can bring success in the engaging of that talent or skill is already present with the person. When you find your passion, and engage with it, you will not labor to be rich and successful. Your passion will attract the success.

We, however, have a situation now where the vast majority

63

of people are working on jobs and vocations that they are completely impassioned towards. They just want to do something and get paid so they can get along from day to day. The business arena is thus filled with millions of people who are completely disconnected from the industries and organizations they work in. Little wonder that one of the major problems companies grapple with is productivity. This is because there is a direct link between passion and performance.

A peculiar reality in my country is the situation where most graduates from either the universities, colleges or technical schools end up jumping at the first offer of employment they receive after a long period of waiting after graduation. For them it's about the pay slip and survival, and much less about contributing to a vision that they are passionate about.

The realization of this as a problem for productivity has forced most big businesses to invest heavily on staff induction and training. This helps to get the employees, who are mostly non-professionals in the core line of the businesses, to learn about and focus on the vision of the business. The positive fall out of this trend is the vibrant and growing corporate and manpower development training services industry around the world.

## Identify Your Passions

Some people are blessed with several talents that they are passionate about at varying degrees. They practically could engage with any and all of these talents and succeed. However, even such a person must learn to identify which of these passions to exploit first that can put him in the best position to eventually work on the other talents in time. Learning to do this will aid the individual in avoiding confusion and frustration. What can you do now that can become the bedrock of your future empire? Ask yourself this question, meditate on it and arrive at your true answer. Most successful business owners of the world today who have business in various economic sectors have a primary business that forms the base from which they venture into all other directions. They guard the primary venture jealously knowing that it is the cash cow that provides the power to project forward.

My very good friend, Ayotunde Stuffman is a multi-award winning young entrepreneur running a multi-million dollar business from Lagos, Nigeria. His company today is one of the foremost indigenous value adding brands in the Telecommunications and Information Technology sphere of business. With operations now in eight countries and about fifty staff members, VAS2Nets is a product of pure passion in motion.

Ayo initially wanted to pursue a career in Medicine as a young boy coming out of high school (I wanted that too). After abandoning the university when he was not admitted to study medicine, Ayo ventured into business to test his entrepreneurial skills. However, because of a setback in the business world he decided to go back to college.

At this point, Ayo's dad brought to his attention that he had watched him and noticed his dexterity with gadgets and computers. Hence, advised my friend to consider studying computer science. The decision to listen to his dad set my friend on the course to become an icon in the Information

Technology sector in Nigeria today, with his influence and business growing beyond Nigeria by the day.

After graduating from college and working as an employee for about five years, Ayo was hungry for more challenges in the sector, because he saw a future that tickled the creativity he possessed. He stepped out of paid employment and in partnership with his wife, Teni, he built a successful business with passion, focus, discipline and the readiness to take calculated risks. Ayo, in just a little over eight years of engagement, has a great lifestyle working on his dreams. His business now renders value added solutions to organizations in different business sectors.

A point you must not fail to take notice of in my friend's story is the fact that his passion was not initially recognized by him as an asset strong enough to build his dreams and fortune on. He had the good fortune of having a father who was observant enough to recognize a talent that could be translated into value in his son.

## Passion Is Transferable

In the late eighties when I was getting set to write my high school graduating exams as a final year student, we had a common problem among the student population. Most students were not doing well in Mathematics, yet it was a compulsory subject to pass to have any hope of getting admission to any tertiary institution of learning.

The complaint among a lot of the students in my school was that the teachers we had teaching the subject, and some other core subjects were not quite good at communicating the knowledge they possessed to the students. Not many of the students would admit that they were also quite dull. I also struggled with math and was really bothered about it becoming a hindrance to my getting into the university.

Like a bolt out of the blue, a young man called, Mr. Iduma, arrived at our school in fulfillment of his one year national service (NYSC), after graduation from the university. He was assigned to take the set of final year students in math. This young man exuded so much confidence, and he would repeatedly announce in class that by the time we had been taught math by him, no sane student in our set would flunk the subject in the coming exams. He would proclaim rather dramatically, his love for mathematics, and wonder why anyone should have problems with the subject.

He made sure he snuck into the different classes in our set of graduating students anytime he noticed that a teacher of some other subject was not in class. He even had us going to school on Saturdays for extra classes! He was clearly obsessed with the thought of his students doing very well in mathematics.

He was so passionate about the subject that within weeks of his arrival at our school, discussions about him and math were the order of the day among both students and teachers. We started comparing notes and working on formulas in class amongst ourselves. At some point my dad asked me if I was studying any of the other subjects I would be taking in the coming exams, and I told him that it was math that I had the most concerns about, so I was giving more time to it.

By the time the results of the exams were out we had such

a high pass rate that we, the students, concluded among ourselves that whoever failed the subject really had a problem with learning. I remember telling my closest friends what my score grade would be just after we finished the paper in the exams. The young teacher had told us we would be able to predict our score at the end of the math exam if we apply ourselves to his teaching method. The grade I predicted was the grade I scored when the results were released.

The young man had successfully transferred his passion for mathematics to us as his students. The plus was that most of the students applied that passion to the other subjects and our school had one of the best results statewide that year. If passion is fire, then you can understand why coal is used to fire even more coal to create energy. Find someone who can transfer passion to you in an area of mutual interest. You don't necessarily have to be the primary source of the passion you apply to succeed. The secondary source is often good enough.

The story of my high school math teacher is a type of countless others that show how role models and mentors can transfer passion to others in practically any field of endeavor. The beauty of this is that the primary source of the passion does not have to be physically or directly involved with the recipient of the transfer. Most adventuring entrepreneurs of today are being inspired by mentors who they have chosen by themselves without such mentors being aware that they have such a mentee. The internet and globalization has made distance mentoring, whether deliberate or passive very easy and millions are tapping into the opportunities available.

A very pertinent truth here is that the pursuit and actualization of our individual dreams and aspirations is our responsibility and we must be accountable for our results.

The decision to harness every faculty and platform that can boost our potential to be successful is ours to make. The resources now available for kindling and engendering passion are practically inexhaustible. If your dream is big enough to count for something and your passion fire is hot enough, you have no limits.

## Protect Your Passion

If there is an undesirable item that is however very common around the world that item will be the dream killer, the wet towel that puts out passion. The energy and fire of passion can so easily be drained off by the negative person who has lost the desire and impetus to aspire and who sees no reason why you should be so energized about your dreams and aspirations. For every mentor and role model out there, there are thousands of dream killers. Little wonder there is yet so much for mankind to accomplish.

Negative people can be so dangerous to passion that as much as is possible we must keep them at a safe distance. This is because the negative, dream killing energy they carry can very readily implant unproductive images and information on our minds that we start to progressively lose our passion. Further exposure to such destructive energy can only result in our ending up where they are, in the doldrums of unbelief. Oftentimes the problem with avoiding dream killers is compounded by the fact that they are all around us! They are family, friends, colleagues at work, church members and so on. They are practically in your face and are ever ready to shoot those ice darts to quench the fire of your passion; 'whatever made you think you can succeed at that business? Don't you remember that your dad and granddad failed at it too?' Then some more; 'your dad's debts are yet to be fully settled and you want to risk the little you have?!'

A good dose of statements like these over a relatively short time frame can definitely take one from being excited about an idea to being deflated and even morose. You lose confidence not just in the idea, but in your abilities too. Self esteem can so readily be turned to self loathing when kept in the care of negative people.

I remember a meeting I had in my third year in the university with my course level adviser. I had noticed from his disposition and tone that day that he was quite dissatisfied about something. Soon enough he came out with it. He told me with so much disdain how a student who had graduated from the department a couple of years prior and who was the son of a rich Nigerian father had come back to employ one of the senior lecturers in the same department to work for that ex-student in the business the rich father had set up for his son.

The point my course level adviser was putting across to me was that there is really no reason to be passionate about anything in this life, if an ex-student can come back and make his former lecturer now address him as a boss. He was so negative in that exchange I had with him that I had to consciously speak to myself in my mind that I was not going to let his disappointment kill my interest in Chemistry as a course, because I was looking forward to becoming a researcher after graduation. Obviously, my plan changed soon after graduation and I became a salesman in the courier services industry.

Therefore, we owe it to ourselves to wear our convictions,

persuasions, and passion deep inside our minds and to guard them really jealously from negative people. You must learn how to give little or no time at all to that person around you who never sees anything good in the world to be grateful for. This is because even the slightest negative image or information that filters into the subconscious mind becomes an issue to be dealt with going forward. It takes more energy and investment to renovate than to build it right at the first.

Aside from negative people, we are also surrounded by negative media and popular culture which have made what used to be the bad become the new good. Print and electronic media are awash with stories of death, disease, famine, lack and poverty, irreligion, immorality and cultural rebellion, which are now the basic components of contemporary entertainment and news. The end result of this kind of exposure on the unsuspecting and unguarded mind is a warped world view and a sense of displacement or dislocation. This further leads to the corruption of the mindset of individuals that paralyses passion and venturing.

## Nurturing Your Passion

Passion is energy, raw energy. The thing about energy is that it cannot be destroyed. It is only converted from one form to another. Energy is also transmitted and can be visualized as waves. What this devolves to is that passion creates an environment around you that must be sustained and nurtured, otherwise it is converted into another form of energy. This often is negative energy like despondency, anxiety, fear or even frustration. For these negative forms of dispassion not to be engendered you must sustain your passion energy.

71

You consolidate your passion by building and maintaining an atmosphere around you that validates your positive emotional attachment to the subject of your passion. Passion rides on emotions to expand but emotions are very tricky in that they are in most cases fleeting. You therefore must become a master of your emotions and channel the right ones towards nurturing your passion rather than the opposite. That is why the most successful people in our world are those who have the characteristics of being emotionally strong. They sustain an atmosphere of excitement and even euphoria towards the subjects of their passions in the face of opposing energies and other contradictions. They arrive at a point where nothing contrary to their passion is given emotional space in their minds and when something slips through the cracks in their mental armor, they quickly gather themselves and reset the atmosphere.

This is why you cannot afford to accommodate negative associations as you go in pursuit of your passion. They will transmit negative energy to you that will progressively depreciate your passion for delivering on your dreams and desires. This is the hard-core reality. Bad communication and association will definitely corrupt good morals and objectives. There is no getting around this principle. Your dreams are your babies and you must become that 'mother' figure that will put up a fight to the death to protect and nurture her babies.

## Feed Your Passion with Knowledge

Another thing to do in nurturing passion is to indulge in information in various forms and from different sources that promote and strengthen your passion fire in the particular area of your interest, talent or endeavor. Going back to my mantra that says 'there is nothing new under the sun, but the same old things can be done differently,' you will always find some existing example of what you are trying to accomplish. It just will not be an exact type of your idea. That is where your individuality will shine forth. Passion that is not nurtured will dissipate.

Imagine yourself on holiday in the woods in a cottage. You have a wood fire burning to keep the cottage warm. The fire is quite boisterous and the wood is crackling at the initial stages. Then after a while you notice that the flames are going down and the fire will soon expire. This is simply because the initial stack of wood that got the fire going is fast burning out. What do you do to keep the fire strong? You throw more wood into the flames before the fire dies out completely. That is the exact same way passion is nurtured. You must keep the flames strong and excited to maintain the desired energy levels to accomplish your goals.

If you are passionate about cars for instance, then you will likely be a collector of magazines and books on cars. You probably will be well acquainted with TV shows and movies about cars. If you are a Real Estate investor you will constantly be on the lookout for any and every piece of information you can find on the Real Estate market in your community. Journals and magazines on the industry will not be strange to you. The money market operator naturally will constantly follow the financial markets around the world daily to be abreast of where the opportunities are in the market. This principle affects all areas of human interest in exactly the same way. Passion drives you in the direction of your desires, goals, and dreams.

73

# Chapter 7

## THE CREATIVE ESSENCE

*"You were created to be a creator!"*
**'Lolu Ogunmade**

I have through time been quite dissatisfied with the status quo in almost every aspect of life. I have desired, and do desire still, an ideal that I see deep within me, and which I strive towards. I cannot accept the observed reality, as I long to bring to bear on myself and by extension, on the world around me, a new experience. I see it and I desire to make it my reality. Everything can be different, and everything can be better. We should never get to the point where we feel that we have accomplished. There are always higher heights to attain in every area of endeavor.

The belief that one has achieved the best possible at any time and in any area of life brings about a sense of complacency. The world requires of us all the commitment to innovation, experimentation and research to elevate the experience of life. Imagine what it would be like for us in the twenty first century to be confronted with the life of people of the first century! Imagine that they were satisfied with the status quo and successfully passed that persuasion to the generations that followed until you and I got here. The reason why this picture of a world that refuses to transform and a people who fail to progress is not acceptable to you is what this chapter addresses.

## You Were Created To Create

This is a fact that you must meditate upon until you experience a mental and emotional rebirth. When this happens, the likely questions you will grapple with such as, 'what am I meant to create?' and 'why is it important for me to create when everything seems to have been done already?' will easily be answered. You will recognize quite clearly that the world thrives on the contributions of all people, whether actively or passively. Furthermore, you will most likely choose to be one that makes things happen rather than one that watches things happen.

The creative essence is that intrinsic presence in each individual, which when connected and properly and purposefully channeled brings about change. This change, first in the individual, leads to a change, by extension, in the world. I must say quite reluctantly that the change can be either positive or negative. This depends on the individual and the energy behind his motivation.

Mankind is described as homo sapiens, which speaks of the extent of development the human mind has in comparison to the animals. Man's ability to think gives him the quality of being proactive rather than just, like the animals, being reactive to situations and circumstances. However, human kind is also described as homo faba, which is indicative of his ability to fabricate and create tools to help him achieve set goals. These two aspects of man reflect the fact that man in his true essence is a creator. The fact that certain primates or apes have been found to, in a rather primitive way, work with crude 'tools' cannot bring them into equality with humans.

Most religious persuasions of the world teach that there is a great and Almighty Creator, who created all things including people. Man is at the top of creation and has the very nature of this Almighty Creator in being able to bring forth things to enhance his life on earth. This creative propensity is present in every human being on the face of the earth. The thing is that each individual has to be able to recognize and understand this power.

The creative essence resides in the subconscious mind and must be activated by a well developed conscious mind to achieve a set purpose. Otherwise, it is subject to external impulses which overtake the subconscious and produce results subject to the received impulses. Simply put, the longer it takes a person to reach the point where he determines what he wants out of life, the longer such a person will be a recipient of whatever life throws at him.

I believe that this is the most important thing this book is meant to communicate to you. The concept of you experiencing a mindshift is to bring you to a point where based on a new set of information and images (knowledge), you decide that it's time for a change in your life. This change then comes through as you tap into the creative essence, the power within you to create the life you have decided to live.

Everything takes off from a decision. If you are convinced that you are not living the life you desire to live, make a decision to create that life that you have identified, and get to work on your subconscious mind until it brings the picture of the life you want to you, in real and tangible terms. This is not going to be an easy do, but it definitely will be worth the effort. Nothing works like a mind that sees no limitations to achieving set goals, and that accommodates no barriers to how big the goals can be.

The failure of the world today is that people have been led to abandon the creative essence resident in each person and to submit their minds to the dictates of others. The average person has had their mind completely overrun by calculated impulses and messages of others who seek to control the thinking of the world, and they actually do. The media is constantly bombarding us with images and voices that hold the ultimate goal of mind control. They seek to control what people think, which affects their attitudes and will determine what they do and how they live.

Now this is not a castigation of the media as an entity, because the media and its functions are a very crucial part of life in today's world. However, mainstream media has become a power and control mechanism in the hands of the established powers of the day. Governments, corporations and even religious bodies now use the media to circulate messages targeted at specific outcomes. This puts a responsibility on the individual to guard and filter the information finding its way into the mind.

# Unlocking Your Creative Essence

The person who wants to live a different life based on the realization that things can be better than they are must agree that:

* I am today the totality of my past decisions.
* No one else, but me can be held responsible for my decisions.
* It is not too late to change things around
* I have the power to change things that I don't want in my life.
* I can create the life I want if I commit to the vision of what that life is.
* I must create and sustain a mind renewal experience through exposure to people, information, and images that enhance my vision of the life I want.

Your complete and total agreement with the above statements is a prerequisite to you going through the experience of a mindshift. Without seeing the absolute truth in these statements, you will not see any need for things in your life and peculiar situation to change and you will not make the decision to effect the changes necessary to move to a higher level of living. The consequence of not making a decision for change is that your subconscious mind will not pull together the information needed to push through a mindshift in you, even when the information is readily available. This is because what you do not passionately desire will eventually be lost, even when it is freely given to you.

One of my mentors in business, whom I have not seen in a long time, though a lawyer by professional qualification, was drawn to creative consultancy. He saw the need for a departure from the norm across the broad spectrum of businesses and industries in Nigeria, and internationally too, in terms of culture, adding value, public perception, and service delivery. He felt deeply that clients or customers deserved a better experience in their brand representation. The enhanced brands would ultimately deliver better bottom lines to the businesses after all.

Therefore, he developed new business models for brand consulting, and began pushing forward his concepts. He soon became one of the most popular and successful brand consultants in Nigeria. In time, he has expanded the coverage of his business into different industries like research, social media and policy consulting and has built a team of highly motivated and engaged staff to serve his clientele.

Today, Alder Consulting and its spin offs and subsidiaries have made Mr. Leke Alder a globally desired consultant. He has an office in London, and has affiliates in several key locations around the world. Mr. Leke Alder simply identified a need in his community and decided to do something about it. He engaged his inherent creative essence and brought forth solutions targeted at the perceived deficiencies in businesses and sold his ideas. He is still doing that today.

I remember one of the sessions I had with him over a decade ago. I was complaining to him about wanting to start a business with an idea that I had then. He told me very clearly that what I needed was not money, but the ability to lay out my ideas clearly. 'The right idea generates its own capital' he said, 'all you need is goodwill' he concluded. He went on to tell me how he started his consultancy with capital which was the advance payment from his first client.

Each of us has the same ability to meet specific needs that exist around us, if only we would look deeply enough to identify not just the need, but our potential to meet it. We all owe the world an obligation to leave it better than we met it. Sadly, most have left the world worse off than they met it, simply because they denied their communities the contributions they could have uniquely made.

Fulfillment in life is tied to a knowing that in any particular aspect of life one has delivered. Like another of my mentors in business puts it, we must go to bed each night having no regrets because we know we delivered the best we could have in the day that is coming to an end. Challenge yourself, find your unique assignment and do the world the great favor of delivering to the best of your ability. And remember, it is not about perfection, but about performance. Refuse to take to the grave that thing within you that will make the world a better place to live in.

## Ideas Have Life

Ideas can be viewed as mind signals and indicators of a possible future. Ideas are born in the mind and nurtured in the mind until they are well developed and eventually acted upon. This means that ideas have life because they are incubated in the mind of a person that is alive. This person may choose to share the idea(s) with others, thereby adding more life to the idea. The energy that grows the idea comes from the energy that keeps the individual alive, and as such the idea lives the life of the one carrying it in his mind.

If the bearer or carrier of an idea does not share the idea

with anyone else and does not activate the idea, such an idea will likely die with the person. Although a semblance of an original idea that a person fails to act on may be inspired in another person's mind, it is usually never exactly the same when this happens. This is due to the uniqueness of each individual.

No one lives in the grave, hence, no idea or vision can live in the grave. Ideas only have life as long as they are borne by a mind that is alive. An idea lives the life of the one who bears that particular idea. Sadly, a lot of great ideas have died and are buried with men and women who did not activate them.

## Ideas Need Collaboration

It is not very difficult to observe that ideas often require collaboration between the vision bearer and other people, and/or institutions. When an idea starts to be executed more inputs are required than the protagonist can singlehandedly produce. This is a fact of life. Therefore, let go of the instinct to do it all alone; this will only very quickly lead to exasperation as the futility of such a stance becomes obvious. There is a reason why you are not alone or all by yourself in the world.

While it is true that the original idea is yours, contributions from others in the specific area of relevance to your efforts will definitely be required to accomplish the set objective and goal. As it is needful for the sun to aid the trees in photosynthesis, so is it needful for the soil to hold up the trees to receive sunlight. The tree, no matter how strong and determined it is, cannot receive sunlight to synthesize its

81

needed carbon dioxide without the soil holding it upright. Likewise, you will get your idea crystallized much faster when you identify that support or collaborative structure particular to your idea.

What this demands is that you must carefully analyze your intentions to identify the support structures suited to your endeavor. You must then engage with the identified supports as is applicable within defined parameters utilizing a plan of action to get your desires accomplished. All of this you must do while protecting the integrity of the original idea, but without being impervious to useful suggestions that can help polish the crude idea. Remember that it is your idea, because you are a unique entity and the idea should bear some semblance to your character traits that are supportive to the success of the idea when crystallized. This is important because some entrepreneurs have seen their original ideas and concepts take up a very unfamiliar outlook by the time they are formed due to the overbearing influences of supposed collaborators.

You must, however, be assured of the fact that you will definitely always find help in bringing your ideas to life. That is the way the world was built to function. It may take some time and effort, but your commitment to the goal, positive mental attitude and passion will draw the help required to you ultimately. Not only this, but if you hold on to your dreams, in time the 'how to', 'when to' and 'where to' questions will be surely answered. I have had to wait and search for fifteen years to get to the point of writing this book.

# Chapter 8

## SOME EXAMPLES OF PEOPLE WHO CHANGED THE WORLD

*"We all have peculiar talents that can be translated into value and delivered to the world."*
**'Lolu Ogunmade**

I want to progress with this work by sharing with you, from my perspective, the stories of some people who in their different generations changed the world in different ways. These are people who through desire backed with passion stuck to their visions of what could be and went the whole hog to unleash their creative essence on the world. They saw opportunities and faced the odds that all men face, but they overcame and they have written their names in the history books and in our minds.

### Thomas Edison

Thomas Edison was born on February 11, 1847 and died on October 18, 1931. An inventor and a business man, among his numerous inventions, he is mostly noted for his invention of the first commercially viable light bulb. Please note that Edison was not the first inventor to create the light bulb. He, however, was the first to get the science and design of a commercially viable light bulb right. This of course stood him out in the field of inventors who worked in this area of an indispensable part of life.

The focus of my discuss on Thomas Edison is the fact that he carried out a thousand experiments before arriving at the design of the light bulb that worked commercially. In just over a year he carried out a thousand experiments to achieve his set goal, a commercially viable light bulb!

Think of all the suggestions he must have received from his own mind and from third parties as he went from one failed trial to another. The voices that advised him to abandon the pursuit would have been so numerous; but he proved his desire to deliver light to the world by going from one failed attempt to the other until finally, he got it right. His desire was tied to the opportunity he saw to be the one who 'gave light to the world.'

When asked eventually how he felt about having failed thousands of times in his attempts to invent, Thomas Edison is reported to have replied saying that he had not failed, but had only found ten thousand ways that the inventions would not work. He is also famously quoted to have said that most people give up on their pursuits and goals just when they are on the verge of success.

## Marie Curie
Marie Curie was born on November 7, 1867, and died on July 4, 1934. She is regarded as the creator of the concept

of radioactivity based on her work in the field of Chemistry. Her discovery of radium and polonium, and her isolation of isotopes brought forth the advent of radiology in medicine during World War 1. This, of course, changed the practice of medicine permanently.

My focus on the contributions of Marie Curie to the world we live in today is from the view point of the sacrifice she made in putting her life at risk, howbeit without realizing the seriousness of what she was exposed to. In her determination to deliver the medical benefits of radioactivity to the world, she exposed herself continuously to the detriment of her health, and she eventually died as a result of over exposure to harmful radioactivity.

I imagine Marie at some point in her research coming to understand that her exposure to the sensitive substances she was working with had become a threat to her life. I also imagine her making the decision to continue with her work until she perfected the outcome of her work for the good of the people of the world. I do not see her sacrifice as being based on the desire to win the two Nobel prizes she was awarded for her work, (the first was jointly awarded to Marie and her husband, and co-researcher, Pierre, in the field of radioactivity), but rather on the need to leave the world a better place.

Nothing in my view exemplifies the power of desire more than the life of Marie Curie. Her desire to impact the world with her creative essence was so strong that it passed down to the next generation as her daughter and son-in-law basically continued from where she stopped at her death.

## Philo T. Farnsworth

He was born on August 19, 1906 and died on March 11, 1971. Philo T. Farnsworth is credited with being the inventor of the electronic television, though he was not the first to explore the possibility of transmitting moving images wirelessly through space and time. He saw the opportunity to be the first to give the world a refined model of the then popularly known mechanical 'televisor', which had been invented years earlier.

Farnsworth worked against the odds of his time and protected his invention with patents, which made it impossible for the economically empowered people in his field to rob him of the benefits of his work. His technology became the basis for all other models made by other scientists in his area of work.

His work and result has changed the world in ways we cannot fathom. The concept of the television could be said to have taken the transmission of messages, whether from the view point of information, news or entertainment, to heights that only those with rich imaginative powers can attain unto.

## The Wright Brothers

The Wright brothers, Orville (August 19, 1871 – January 30, 1948) and Wilbur (April 16, 1867 – May 30, 1912), are the two people to whom the invention of the first fixed wing flying aircraft is credited. They were, notably, not the first to build a flying machine, but were the first to actually invent an aircraft with controls and fixed wings.

Their invention obviously changed the world of aviation

research and engineering, and their engine design is still the basis for all fixed wing aircraft till today. Aviation technology and engineering have definitely improved through the last century, but the bar the Wright brothers set is still the standard.

Picture the countless failed trials that the brothers faced through time as they experimented with various designs of the 'flying machine' and the frustration that could have developed in their minds. Merge this with all the negative reports coming out from failed attempts by others in the same field of research across the aviation world. Imagine the cacophony of voices singing the 'man is not meant to fly' mantra.

The only thing that could have kept the brothers going with their eyes fixed squarely on the goal is a strong desire. Desire so strong that it drowned all the negative voices by playing in the ears and minds of the brothers the sound of the engine of an aircraft in flight designed and built by them.

Today, the concept of human flight is taken for granted and we have developed it so much that man is now flying beyond the ozone into outer space.

## Henry Ford

Henry Ford was born on June 30, 1863 and died on April 7, 1947. The father and pioneer of the modern automobile obviously changed the world in ways he could hardly have imagined on the outset of his innovative quest. That same change he ignited has continued to these present times. Ford was not the first to build a gas-powered engine, but his vision to build a horseless self-propelling carriage formed the basic impetus for his achievement.

His experience on various jobs involving working with machinery and even electricity fueled by his love for machinery of different types also positioned him for his eventual decision to pursue the concept of self-propelling horseless carriages. His first invention, the Quadricycle, became a stepping stone to his first successful automobile. Through the two decades that followed, following basically his desire to make better and cheaper vehicles to maintain, Henry Ford found investors and workers to aid in the actualization of his plans.

He was a dogged fighter that kept his dream in focus and kept every opposing idea at bay in his pursuit of his goals. Eventually, after several failures along the way, Henry Ford brought the first full scale assembly line into the production of his vehicles, and by 1922, half of the cars on American roads were Ford model Ts. By this time too, he had made many millionaires out of his investors and had a well paid workforce that was committed to the high turnover of vehicles the company was producing.

Try to imagine our world today without the myriads of brands and designs of automobiles. It's a pretty odd picture, right? Whether they are cars, trucks, SUVs and even more professional automobile based technical vehicles, they were all arguably inspired by the work of Henry Ford and the assembly line production model.

He was not the sharpest business mind of his day having had very little formal education, but he was a man with vision who was not going to stop at anything short of accomplishing that set objective. He is famous for his doggedness, which saw him practically directly run the Ford Motor Company, the largest in the world then, right until just before his death. He saw something most people in his day could not see, because his mindset was different.

Henry Ford is famously quoted to have said that 'If the people set their minds on anything, it is impossible to prevent their getting what they want.' He surely got what he wanted.

## Martin Luther King Jr.
Martin Luther King Jr. was born on January 15, 1929 and was assassinated on April 4, 1968. He was an American Baptist Church minister, humanitarian, activist, and also an African-American civil rights movement leader. He is the most celebrated African-American male leader of the civil rights movement era in the United States of America, particularly in the period between the 1950s till the turn of the decade in 1970.

The main throng of Martin Luther King Junior's life was based on his belief that the world at large and the United States of America in particular, would be a much better place if all men were truly treated equally in all aspects of life. Racism from any and indeed every perspective must be done away with and we must all embrace the diversity of humanity. The end of slavery in the United States, which became status quo by the end of the American civil war in May of 1865 supposedly meant that all people should have been treated as equals.

However, racial segregation in the southern states of the union particularly, but also evident in different modes across the country continued for almost a century. Thus, the agitations and activism aimed at correcting the anomaly arose across the country. Different groups and organizations sprung up all over the country with different strategies to fight for civil rights for all.

Martin Luther King Jr. began his activism early in his career as a Baptist minister, and by the mid 1950s had become well known leading up to the 1955 Montgomery Bus Boycotts, which he led. His activism went forward through the years till the 1963 march on Washington DC where he gave the world famous 'I have a dream...' speech. In the speech, he expressed his ideal picture of the America he hoped to help bring to the fore. This, of course, became his most famous speech and established him as one of America's best orators.

He went on to win the Nobel Peace Prize in 1964 for his nonviolent approach to civil disobedience as the pivotal strategy of his activism life. He believed and spread the idea of a nonviolent way of demonstrating dissent and disagreement with the governments across America, both at local and federal levels. His stand point was not to engage with the authorities at the same level of violence and brutality, which were the hallmarks of the states' reaction to activism. He believed in putting forward an argument without descending to violence and destruction of lives and property.

Martin Luther King Jr. continued with this approach all through his years as an activist up until 1968 when he was planning another march on Washington D.C, but was assassinated in April of the same year. His unique and principled stance towards activism, which he maintained all through his time as an activist won him many post humus awards. Many land marks, counties, and streets in the United States, and other places around the world have been named after him as a recognition and validation of his ideals and world view.

He stands today as only the second American in history to have his birthday celebrated every year as a national holiday.

## Nelson Mandela

Nelson Mandela was born on July 18, 1918, and died on December 5, 2013. Although he was not the father of the anti-apartheid struggle in South Africa, he definitely became the face of the struggle, because of his peculiar role in the cause.

Though racial segregation had been practiced in South Africa by the minority white settlers for over a century the official political instrument of apartheid was introduced by the National Party in 1948. This stricter form of racial segregation gave the government powers to practically put down any form of an uprising from the native people of the land against the policies of the government.

This was the country that Nelson Mandela grew up in. As a matter of fact, the name Nelson was given to him by his school teacher because it had become a practice to give the children English names to replace their tribal names. The young Nelson, the first child in his family to be formally educated grew through elementary school to high school, and eventually got admitted into the only university for black students then in the country. His activist tendencies had already begun and he was sent packing from the university with some of his friends the following year for challenging some of the school's policies.

Mandela moved to Johannesburg to find work and eventually finished his bachelor's degree by correspondence. He got his law degree thereafter and the human rights activist in him got him and some friends into the African National Congress (ANC) in 1944. He also married his first wife in the same year. They had four children together before their divorce in 1957. By this time Mandela and his friend Oliver Tambo had become integral parts of the ANC and were leading the youth wing of the party which was in direct opposition to the policy of apartheid of the National Party.

Mandela and Tambo started the first ever black and minorities law firm to assist victims of the apartheid policy of the government at low cost. He championed the policies and strategies of the ANC through the early days encouraging above all, the use of nonviolent civil disobedience and the campaign for the Defiance of Unjust Laws. His first major clash with the government occurred in 1956 when Mandela and many others were arrested and tried, but were eventually acquitted in 1961.

However, his nonviolent stance changed in 1960 after the Sharpeville massacre in which sixty nine members of the ANC and PAC (Pan Africanist Congress), a splinter group of the ANC, were murdered by agents of the government. Mandela and other leaders of the congress went underground and engaged other radical approaches to fight against apartheid. The armed resistance, thus, began and took the struggle to a new dimension.

In 1962, after several years of armed struggle, which included guerilla war training outside the country and the attraction of the attention of the international community, Mandela and many leaders of the congress, some white activists inclusive, were arrested. They were tried for eight months in the Rivonia trials. He and seven others were eventually given life imprisonment sentences. This marked the beginning of his twenty-seven year imprisonment.

Throughout the time he spent in solitary confinement in prison, seventeen years of which he spent on the famous Robben Island maximum security facility, Mandela maintained his stand on the issue of race equality and human rights. As his friend Oliver Tambo, who had earlier escaped into exile mounted an international campaign that pressured the South African government to abolish the policy of apartheid, Mandela still led the struggle from behind bars. He was later moved to a lower security level prison on the mainland. Due to pressures on the government, he was offered several deals to make him denounce the struggle for freedom to get released but he refused repeatedly.

By 1989, then President F. W. De Klerk, who had been elected in 1988 unbanned the ANC and called for national reconciliation. After some secret negotiations, De Klerk ordered the release of Nelson Mandela on February 11, 1990. Mandela went on to unify several opposition political organizations under the umbrella of the ANC and won the Presidential election of April 26, 1994. He was inaugurated as the first black president of South Africa on May 10, 1994.

Mandela served as president for five very eventful and transformative years in South Africa and retired from politics in 1999 after marrying Graca Marchel, his third wife, in 1998. His second marriage to Winnie had ended in divorce six years earlier in 1992. Now out of the political arena Mandela spent the rest of his life promoting international efforts to promote peace, human rights and equality across the globe. He also championed the campaign against AIDS in South Africa and worldwide, and started several organizations to promote his causes.

As he advanced in age, Mandela became stricken with several health challenges, which he battled with just like he battled against apartheid. He eventually died due to a recurring lung infection. Mandela is highly celebrated globally for his tenacity and resolve in the pursuit of his chosen ideals. He was also in December of 1993 jointly awarded the Nobel Peace Prize alongside former President F. W. De Klerk. He was indeed a global citizen and the United Nations in 2009 declared July 18 'The International Nelson Mandela Day.' The day is marked every year in recognition of Mandela's contributions to the world at large.

No other individual has affected the world, in these modern times, quite like Nelson Mandela.


## Sir Richard Branson

He was born on July 18, 1960. This British business mogul who is worth about five billion dollars, based on the Forbes list for the year 2015, makes my list of people who have changed the world. The perspective from which I want to discuss his impact on our world today is entrepreneurship.

Growing up in Surrey, England with Dyslexia, Richard Branson struggled through school until he eventually dropped out at age sixteen to start his first business, a magazine called

Student to serve the interests of students in his community. This was the first major indicator of the great entrepreneur that the young man was at heart. He raised eight thousand dollars in 1966 in advertisement payments to fund the first edition of the magazine and gave out the fifty thousand copies printed for free.

Branson eventually decided to leverage on the rock music culture of the time to start a mail order record sales business, which is how Virgin Music was born. He went from just selling records to opening a recording studio of his own, which took his business to another level entirely. His ability to deal and to attract the bands he worked with and made successes of made Virgin Records one of the top six record companies in the world in less than ten years.

However, like most entrepreneurs, Branson did not always make the right investment decisions and as such he had some business failures along the path to success and the billionaire life. He had to sell Virgin Records in 1992, which was a tough call for him in his effort to keep the other Virgin businesses afloat, including Virgin Atlantic, his airline. He always found a way to bounce back though and eventually got back into the music business in 1996 with Virgin Radio and V2, his new record company.

Sir Richard Branson went on to start other businesses in different fields of interest and now has over two hundred companies in the Virgin Group in more than thirty countries. His most recent and very popular venture is in the area of space tourism with Virgin Galactic. The very adventurous fun loving disposition of Sir Richard Branson reflects in his choice of business pursuits and the style associated with his companies. Nevertheless, he is a focused entrepreneur who is always ready to battle any established opposition to his business interests. This fighting spirit is also reflected in his sports life and world record breaking stunts like crossing oceans in hot air balloons, and going around the world in a hot air balloon.

Sir Richard Branson is an entrepreneur in a class by himself. He is the classical think-out-of-the-box business man, who is never afraid to take risks, but who also takes only calculated risks. He is quoted to have said 'a business has to be involving, it has to be fun and it has to exercise your creative instincts.' Richard Branson definitely believes in doing business and making money, but he also believes in having fun all through the journey and giving back to the world through various causes and charities.

## Bill Gates

William Henry 'Bill' Gates III was born on October 28, 1955. The Seattle, Washington born business magnate is said to be worth almost ninety billion dollars by Forbes in its 2015 list. Bill Gates, in my view and in the context of this book, is probably the most iconic example of the duplicator who became more successful and celebrated than the innovator. He neither created the ideas of personal computers, nor the idea of software. He just saw the vast opportunity in both areas of information technology and positioned himself early to rule in that arena.

His interest in computers was clearly established by the time he was thirteen years old, and by the time he was ready for college he surprised his parents by not going in to study law, but chose to pursue programming and software development. He went into business with his high school friend Paul Allen in 1970 and they made their first sale worth twenty thousand dollars to write a program for the traffic management of the city of Seattle. Bill Gates was fifteen years old then. He went on to finish high school and got into Harvard, but continued his pursuit of programming.

In 1975 Gates and Allen formed their company Microsoft to serve the need of their growing clientele with a particular contract at hand then. The business went through some hard times, but the two friends kept at it and sharpened their knowledge and business management skills, with Bill Gates positioning as the spokesperson of the company and the CEO. By 1979, with twenty-five employees, the company made two and a half million dollars. Bill Gates was just twenty three years old. The company grew rapidly from then on, and by 1981 with a hundred and twenty eight staff, the company's revenue grew to sixteen million dollars.

Based on the business tactics of Bill Gates and his strong mindset in the face of litigations and criticisms in the business environment, the company by 1985 had thirty percent of computers in the world running on its software. By 1986 when the company went public Bill Gates became a multimillionaire, and by 1999 Bill Gates was worth just over a hundred billion dollars. All of this was accomplished by Gates based on a vision of what the world could become with the advent of personal computers, and what the creator of the operating system running those computers stands to gain in business profits.

This vision became the underlying strength for the battles he fought through time to establish Microsoft as the iconic business it has become today. That same vision has given Bill Gates the leverage to be one of the most benevolent donors to several causes around the world today through the Bill and Melinda Gates Foundation. Having separated himself from the daily running of Microsoft fully in 2008, Bill Gates now travels the world with his wife, Melinda, giving from his great wealth to the needy across the globe.

The world now runs, arguably, on Microsoft Windows and stores information in the Microsoft Cloud. It would surely be a different world without Bill Gates and Microsoft.

Even though I have chosen to highlight the impact of these few people on our world through different periods of time to the present day, there remain countless others who have and are changing our world positively. You have some names ringing through your mind now that are not on the list I have given above, I am sure of it. I have selected these ones based on my personal appreciation of the changes their work has delivered to the world in the different areas of human life and endeavor they engaged. Imagine our world without the electric light bulb, television, radioactivity, telecommunications, aviation, equality and human rights, racial equality, entrepreneurial spirit, and information technology. It does not look like a very bright picture, right?

That is why it is very important for each of us to discover our peculiar talents and impact the world with them. I want to reiterate here that each one of us alive today has some unique quality or talent if you will, that can be translated into value. Value when delivered to the world through a system attracts commensurate rewards in financial, social, emotional, and material terms. It all depends on our ability to recondition our minds utilizing new information, images and experiences. Get to work! The world is waiting for you.

# Chapter 9

## A NEW PERSON; A NEW WAY

"Today is experience, the future is life."
**'Lolu Ogunmade**

In the earlier chapter on 'Thoughts and Imaginations', I made mention of our children. My wife and I are blessed with the most wonderful girl and boy twins. The short version of the story is something like this.

My wife and I were married in August 1999. After waiting as planned for a couple of years, we began working on building a family, but we did not conceive when we expected to. Eventually, we decided to seek medical counsel to know what the issues were and what path to tread going forward. After some more years of different procedures and treatments, I became fed up with the pain and embarrassing situations my wife, particularly, was exposed to, and I put an end to the medical approach.

I desired a solution of course, but I closed my mind against another doctor's appointment. All the while my wife was undergoing treatment for the side effects of the earlier procedures. She kept requesting that I should change my mind and let us engage the doctors again. By this time, it was nine years after we got married and I went back to the doctor with her only to be told that we needed assisted conception to be parents. This was an unacceptable reality for me, because, though, I was quite familiar with the scientific advances in the field, I never saw us going down that path.

I look back now and realize that I went through a subtle, yet tough mindshift for the next two years, during which information from different sources got me to the point of deciding to go ahead with it. The information that brought about my mindshift came in different deposits from my wife's point of view and pleas, from medical professionals, and quite substantially, from our pastor.

Thus, by the time the last consultant we saw in Nigeria told us that he was more comfortable with us using a surrogate mother, (something our family doctor had been saying for more than a year), though I said no again, I knew it was going to happen just that way. Our pastor advising us to go the surrogate route if need be, without prior knowledge that the consultant had so advised, was the final push I needed.

We left Nigeria to India in 2010, right at the end of March, ten and a half years into our marriage, based on our family doctor's advice that we stood a better chance based on our history, in an environment that possessed better technologyatamoreconvenientcost.Bythistime,Ihadbecomea totally different person in comparison to who I a couple of years earlier. I was ready to experiment with the doctors and other professionals involved in our pursuit of parenthood and I had become more curious. My wife, of course, was more curious than I, and was just eating up every bit of information she could find on the different aspects of the treatment we were about to undertake.

We arrived in India, and exactly two years after, with my wife staying in the country for twenty of the twenty four months, and with nine trips to and from India for me, we arrived back home to Nigeria finally with six weeks old twins, a girl and a boy.

A mindshift when experienced can cause such a transformation that the individual could actually become unrecognizable to people who are connected to the person. I remember my wife used to look at me queer at times and ask me for an explanation of my change from the man that would not even see a doctor to a man who not only agreed to In Vitro fertilization with surrogacy, but agreed to going out of our country for as long as it took to be successful.

## Desire
Complacency and becoming distraught based on unsuccessful attempts to achieve set goals personally or based on another's experience are two destinations you do not want to arrive at or even visit. I spoke about passion in an earlier chapter of this book. Passion rides on desire, because there will be no need for passion if there is no object of desire to be accomplished. Desire is engendered by thinking, which is in itself, a function of the subconscious mind that must become predominant in your consciousness.

The concept of mindshift is such a powerful phenomenon, yet it can only become a reality when its possibility is embraced. The transformative impact of a mindshift is to be desired by anyone who desires a new and higher level of life and living. Understanding that everything can be better than what the status quo reflects puts the need for new information to be received and digested clearly in view. This will open up the mind to innovation deriving from new perspectives and mindsets. The individual who will have this experience however must seek the information that will deliver the objective.

## Desire Must Be Tested and Proven

It is commonly said that the proof of desire is pursuit. The validation of the existence of a true desire channeled towards any objective is the readiness and willingness of the individual concerned to do whatever is necessary to bring that objective to light. Similarly, the reader of this book, who agrees with me that a change needs to occur to bring about a new and higher level of living for him must therefore make a quality decision to seek out relevant information. This information when digested by the subconscious mind in the process of time will deliver the mindshift required to bring about that pre-determined change for the individual.

Desire is something that is readily mouthed countless times in myriads of circumstances every day. However, the weakness of majority of the expressed desires is very easily observed in the passion and commitment, or lack thereof, displayed by people. We live in a world that pays lip service to the ideal while living in the mediocre. The law of attraction teaches that you attract what you are passionate and truly emotional about, what you put out into the world around you. I dare say that this is just a corollary of the universal principle that teaches that what you sow is what you reap.

In every day issues of life, we do not always get what we want when we want it. The same holds true in desiring the experience of a mindshift as a vehicle to a better existence. You probably will not go through a consummate mindshift just from reading this book the first time, but seeds of desire and a recognition of what has been missing in your life will definitely be realized. Deliberately reading this book repeatedly and collecting similar information in the area of your specific interest will definitely and eventually birth in you a mindshift.

You will, for yourself, answer the question of the proof of desire by deliberately embarking on the search for the information and images that will impact your subconscious mind progressively to get you finally to the point of your mindshift. It may not be a smooth ride, but you will be glad you took the journey when you arrive at your destination; the real 'you' that you have looked for all this while. That is the 'you' that the world has been waiting for to fulfill the unique assignment peculiar to you. The importance of this lies in the understanding that to change the world and anything else around you, the change must start with you. You must change before you can change anything and anyone.

## Opportunity
Spring is that season of the year when flowers of different

plants open up their petals to give the attraction to insects to get the sweet nectar they desire. The coming of spring, thus, presents an opportunity for the insects to feed. Underlying this opportunity however, is nature's plan for the pollination of those same flowers so that fruits can grow. A furtherance of nature's plan of serial opportunities is the embedding of the seeds that will keep the species of different plants going forward in the fruits in most cases. When the fruits are eaten or when they decay, the seeds end up in the earth, thus, giving yet another opportunity for that plant species to regenerate. A cycle of serial opportunities thus exists in nature which keeps the equilibrium in place on earth.

In the same way, man is blessed with repeated opportunities on an ongoing basis every day. The sad truth is that the wrong conditioning of people's minds makes recognizing the opportunities around us in any area of our particular interest almost impossible, or it makes actualizing identified openings seem not worth the effort. The world however only rewards and applauds the ones who by engaging with identified opportunities create yet more opportunities for themselves and others too.

Experiencing a mindshift should bring us to the point where we wake up each new day expecting to find at least one unique opportunity to get entangled with to make the world and our life a better one. The farmer who works his field creates not only the opportunity for us to get food but also the opportunity for employment at different levels to be created for people. The business owning entrepreneur not only creates job opportunities for people but also gives opportunities for families to be fed and for children to be schooled. A government that creates a commodious environment for the people by putting infrastructure in place creates myriads of opportunities that will impact the GDP (Gross Domestic Product) of such a country.

Mr. Richard del Rosario mentored me in the direct selling opportunity that I am a part of currently. He always likes to tell his story of how he got into the business just over four years ago. Richard was an executive, back then, in one of the biggest and most popular search engines on the internet. He was comfortable with his six figure annual pay package over there in New York.

He was exposed to an opportunity to live a life that was focused on achieving his own dreams as opposed to what he was doing at the time. As Richard puts it, the gentleman that showed him the opportunity got his attention when he asked him what his 'plan B' was if he could no longer work for the search engine. Richard had never heard of a plan B, and therefore had no such plan.

The realization that his lifestyle and domestic equilibrium with his wife and children would be in jeopardy if he should suddenly lose his employment got him to seriously listen to the gentleman. After listening to what was shared with him and considering the figures presented to him as possible incomes, Richard says he knew this was the business to do. However Richard's ego got in the way and told him not to go from being a well paid executive to become 'the coffee guy!'

He thought about the fact that Mr. Joseph Wilson who had shown him the new business opportunity was already a millionaire in partnership with the company. He also thought about the lifestyle of freedom that Mr. Wilson and others in business with the company lived, and how they were

Mindshift

impacting other lives. This, I dare say, was the point of his mindshift. Richard partnered with the company knowing that he possessed the influence and leverage needed to get his business going. His very best friend laughed at him when he muted the idea of them partnering to build the beverage merchandizing business he was starting.

Richard kept his focus on the opportunity and its possibilities; and just three months into his engagement with the business, he gave up his job with the search giant and went full time with his dream. Mr. Richard del Rosario belongs to the top four hundred in a distributorship of well over a million people spread across fifty one countries and growing.

In just over four years of being in the business, Richard now has a potential earnings ratio of over eight times above his annual pay package on the old job. He tells me repeatedly that he could not have doubled his earnings on the job in the same period if he had stopped himself from embracing the coffee opportunity. The icing on the cake is the fact that he gets to travel the world and help make other people's lives better. He gets to be the one now showing people that the dreams they grew up nursing can still be achieved, if only they learn to embrace new thinking.

Life and living thrive on opportunities, because opportunities keep the world going round. Search for your unique opportunity and use it to give the world even more opportunities.

## Success
Success only demands thinking. The simplicity of this truth

106

is perhaps the reason why most do not recognize it. We have been trained and have possibly trained ourselves to expect to pay a high price for success and the unwillingness to be tasked beyond our comfort zones, which is a pre-requisite anyway, robs us of the zeal to aspire for success. Thus, we fantasize about success and wish for it without being ready to invest the thoughts needed and to act on those thoughts. If on the other hand, another perspective that presents success as a fascinating adventure of self-discovery, development and expression is presented to us, we may be more accommodating to the concept. This is simply because we naturally tend towards the easy rather than the tasking.

Success is almost unbelievably low priced, yet it is rare, because it gives itself only to those who are willing to invest in creative thinking and to commit to actualizing their thoughts. You seek to be comfortable in life generally because that is the way we all are created, we are creatures of comfort. You, thus, create a comfort zone for yourself in every aspect of life that you subconsciously defend aggressively. The issue here is that the success you desire is always outside of your established comfort zone so you will have to get 'uncomfortable' to attain your desire. The payoff is in the fact that you will by getting outside of your comfort zone achieve success and end up in a better comfort zone. Therefore, if your sights are set on the comforts and lifestyle that will come with your working for a higher degree of success, you will most likely be more energized to pursue this new goal.

I will, therefore, say to you that if you helped five families to achieve a better standard of living last year, work towards helping twenty families this year. If you made a million dollars last year, work towards three million dollars this year. If you lost five pounds in weight last month maybe losing eight pounds should be just appropriate this month, if that will not endanger your health in anyway. You had two weeks of vacation last year? You should work towards four weeks of vacation this year, and six to eight weeks next year. Think of anything you have achieved before and push for a higher level of achievement in that area.

Are you hearing that loud voice in your head saying 'who does this guy think he is?!' Does he know how tough it is to even do what I do to get through each day?!' That voice in your head is the very reason why I have written this book and why you are reading it now. That is the non-supportive and preconditioned subconscious mind that we need to renew for you to achieve at your best potential. Take note of this, it's going to take some effort. Once accomplished however, it will deliver satisfaction to you and others in more ways than I can count, because success is attracted to those who are willing to be different.

The choice to keep looking over the fence into your successful neighbor's garden and to become envious, critical, and even self-loathing for having lost your self esteem will always exist. Alternatively, you can choose to look deep inside and tap your creative essence to discover your peculiar talent and learn to exploit it to deliver value to the world. Success is about giving value and getting rewarded in direct proportion to the utility you deliver. If you give the world what it demands and requires you will be very handsomely rewarded and successful, and that refers not only to monetary success. I say this because influence in a lot of situations is more important than cash.

## The Entrapment of Success

The downside of success that is not backed up with the proper mindset is that success has a nasty penchant of making you forget what you did to become successful in the first place! You must have heard stories about people or even companies that were very successful, but are now nowhere to be found. In most cases, the reason is because they somewhere along the line left off discipline and consistency in the context of whatever the secret of the success was and rather focused on living large. They let the cash cow out of the barn while they were 'out painting the town red.'

You could become so distracted by the success that you achieve that you lose it based on several mentality weaknesses and vulnerabilities. With personal success, substance abuse, faulty lifestyle choices, and bad or ill-advised investments are the common entrapments of success. In some other instances, outright illegalities practiced by the individuals or organizations concerned has been the basis for the loss of the attained success.

In the instance of inherited riches or wealth, if the inheritance is passed on to a descendant who is not in the right mindset needed for wealth sustenance, and who does not deliberately seek help, the wealth will most definitely be lost. It is just a matter of time. The thing is that there is no circumventing the universal laws of success, wealth creation and sustenance. This is why a mindshift holds with it the potential to put you in the best position to manage success and to utilize the influence that success avails you.

Influence carries with it more value than cash, because a man wielding it can get all the cash he needs without a dime coming from his personal reserves. On the other hand, you can only have so much personal cash and if you are the big-time business man, then you will always need more cash than you own or directly control. Build your influence base and you can become more successful than you can imagine. Influence rules when all other parameters are aligned properly and it never fails to deliver on its promise.

## Going forward

I said at the beginning of this book that this is my story, my search for who I was created to be and what I need to do (or to know) to become that person. This is important to me, not only from the point of view of personal fulfillment, but from the big picture perspective, what I am supposed to add to the world. This is not an attempt to be noble on my part. It is a product of true inspiration and introspection.

You can find yourself in this picture, my picture. This is simply because my quest is the quest of everyone alive today who has even the faintest idea of what it means to accomplish, to apprehend. The principles shared in this book and expressed through the different stories are universally tested. They have been found to be true irrespective of what the scenario being considered entails. The laws holding the entire universe together are made up of these very principles. The law of cause and effect commands that the laws produce for you, if you invest the effort of learning and mastering these principles so that you can apply them to your peculiar situation.

In the very first chapter where I talked about new think-ing I suggested that traditional patterns of thought are almost entirely irrelevant in today's world within a certain context. I find that even nature presents us with this fact every day. As parents, we often gather with other parents and talk about how our children born into today's world are more advanced in their cognitive traits and attitudes than we were in our days as children. Nothing more than this observation, I guess, buttresses the fact that new thinking is required for life in our world now more than ever before. New thinking centered on new information results in mindshift, which subsequently births new attitudes and a new mindset.

There is no doubt in my mind that your resolve to pursue mindshift will be challenged by the same negative energies you are trying to overcome. Keeping your thoughts, emotions, and actions centered on the object of your desire is the strongest defense you possess in this on-going battle. I call it the battle of the mind. I did write a song with that title back in the university, which the musical band I was then a member of, performed in the campus fellowship, I think in 1993. Yes, I sing too.

Remember that the established systems in the arenas of education, sports, business and even government do not necessarily throw opportunities at you by design. You may, however, by keeping your passion fired up persuade your subconscious mind to embrace your dreams. This creates energy that goes ahead of you to create the circumstances that your dreams become the answers to. Therein is your opportunity to deliver value to the world and get rewarded in commensurate measure.

As you journey onwards, I recommend that you keep these principles at the centre of your meditations, until your subconscious mind accepts the reality of these truths and bestows them on your conscious mind. Then will you be positioned to deliver your utmost potential to our world, because then you would have gone through the needed experience of a mindshift.

I wish you grace, riches and success.

www.ingramcontent.com/pod-product-compliance
Lightning Source LLC
Chambersburg PA
CBHW072238290326
41934CB00008BB/1340